The
BLUE
JEAN
JACKET

The
BLUE
JEAN
JACKET

How Abandonment Affects Your
Health, Wealth, and Relationships

Rena Perozich

THE BLUE JEAN JACKET

© 2025 Rena Perozich

Cover Design and Layout | www.wendykwalters.com

Published by B & B Publishing, LLC | Fairmont, West Virginia

Printed in the USA

ISBN (paperback): 979-8-9992217-1-1

ISBN (hardback): 979-8-9992217-2-8

ISBN (EPUB): 979-8-9992217-3-5

LCCN: 2025912818

DISCLAIMER

This book is a personal memoir and reflects the author's individual experiences, perspectives, and recollections. It is not intended to diagnose, treat, or provide medical or psychological advice or counseling. Readers are encouraged to seek the guidance of qualified health professionals regarding any physical, mental, or emotional health concerns. Any actions taken based on the content of this book are solely at the reader's discretion and risk.

TO CONTACT THE AUTHOR
renaperozich.com

A NOTE TO THE READER

Although I have been involved in pastoral ministry and Christian pastoral counseling for many, many years, I am not a licensed mental health counselor, therapist, or medical professional, and this book should not be used as a substitute for professional support or treatment.

The experiences described in this book are drawn from my own life. I have researched this subject extensively, and I present this material as a lay person who has experienced the effects of childhood abandonment and childhood emotional neglect and found a path toward healing.

Because my studies have spanned more than a decade and literally include dozens of authors, podcasters, articles, journals, and videos, it is impossible for me to remember and give appropriate credit to every thought. When you study a subject over time—particularly one that has captured your interest but you never considered writing about—the information becomes part of you. It gets hard to remember where you learned what and from whom. I have done my best to give honor where honor is due and worked diligently to cite my sources. I have also provided an extensive bibliotherapy at the back of this book to encourage further study by the reader.

A NOTE OF GRATITUDE

To everyone who stood beside me on the winding journey of creating The Blue Jean Jacket—How Abandonment Affects Your Health, Wealth, and Relationships, my heart is brimming with gratitude. This book was not written in isolation; it is the result of countless conversations, shared stories, encouragement, and steadfast support.

Thank you to the friends, family, and mentors who offered wisdom when I faltered and strength when I doubted. Your belief in this project made each page possible. To the experts, authors, artists, and photographers who shared their knowledge, gifts, and experiences, your openness illuminated the many faces of abandonment, allowing this book to offer both authenticity and hope.

To my readers, your desire to understand and heal has been my inspiration from the very beginning. May these words create a space for reflection, compassion, and growth in your own lives. Together, let us continue exploring how our past shapes our present—and, above all, how resilience is born from even the most difficult stories.

With sincere thanks,

—Dr. Rena Perozich

SPECIAL THANKS

Some people have gone above and beyond, and I wanted to mention them by name, as this would have never happened without each of them.

- **Samantha Blevins**, the long hours you sat and listened to my dreams and crazy ideas that I would run past you at all hours, for beach time that always ended up being work time, for sitting at the dining room table and going through literally over a hundred books to help me cite what I wanted to say, for putting up with all the big emotions when this cathartic work became more than I could handle—thank you. All done. Ready to get to work on the next book?

- **Melissa Pierce**, for editing after the editing and then re-editing everything I write, this book included, thank you. You are a gift to me, along with **Carol Jones**, for her advertising and IT work, and encouragement. What a great team God supplied me with. I love you dearly.

- **Breanna Siniscal**, you always have a way of bringing my dreams to life. I share my vision of what I want things to look like, and you bring it to life. I pray that you and your husband's business take off and bless the world. I absolutely love my cover; it showcases my true West Virginia girl colors and how a new life can be built, brick by brick.

JSINISCALPHOTO.COM

- **Shemary Jones Rudash**, what a wonderful time we spent together talking about and taking photos of what my readers now see with their own eyes. You have an eye for creativity that was able to bring to life what I wanted my photos to convey. I feel as though I can give my readers a glimpse into my soul, not just see an author, but the person who wrote the book, and have the feeling that they know me as a friend.

COMPASS30.COM

- **Dr. Keith Johnson**, I'm not sure how it all happened, but the 83K Nation class I took completely rocked my world. I loved it—hated it—loved you—hated you—enrolled in the doctoral program at Destiny College and earned my doctorate degree, and somehow found "My One Word—Abandonment." It was a rollercoaster journey that I never would have gotten on without your personal interest in my life. Thank you.

DRKEITHJOHNSON.COM

PRAISE FOR THE BLUE JEAN JACKET

In *The Blue Jean Jacket,* Rena Perozich opens her heart and invites all of us on a courageous journey through the shadowlands of abandonment and neglect toward authentic healing, wholeness, and hope. With vulnerable honesty and grace-filled wisdom, she comes alongside us and guides us in confronting difficult truths, not merely as a path of insight, but as an essential step toward deep transformation.

This is far more than a memoir; it's a pastoral companion that recognizes the sacredness of every wounded soul's story. Rena reveals how abandonment shapes our very sense of self, yet insists powerfully that these painful experiences do not define us. Through practical tools and heartfelt reflections, she offers pathways toward healing, restored relationships, and freedom from limiting beliefs that hold so many of us captive.

As a shepherd who has walked with many through valleys of trauma, I deeply appreciate the gift Rena is giving us in her transparency: she gives us herself. Her story and insights are balm to any and all who feel forgotten, offering assurance that no wound is beyond the reach of God's healing grace. Her final message is a foundational truth to anchor each and every one of us:

> *"You are not forgotten. You are not forsaken.*
> *You are held in love."*

May this beautifully courageous work become a trusted guide for many on their path toward healing, wholeness, and lasting peace.

—Bishop Mark J. Chironna, Ph.D.
MARK CHIRONNA MINISTRIES | MARKCHIRONNA.COM

We have known Rena Perozich for years as a leader, teacher, entrepreneur, wife, and sister in the Lord. But do we ever truly know the depths someone has walked through to become who they are? In this extraordinary journey, Rena opens her heart and soul, inviting us into a story that is both heartbreaking and hope-filled.

As a child forced to grow up too soon, she bore the weight of responsibility for her siblings, yet she never allowed those experiences to define her. With unwavering courage and deep faith, Rena reveals how God met her in the darkest places and turned her pain into purpose.

This is more than a story of survival—it is a declaration of victory. Her life echoes the words of Joseph in Genesis 50:20: "You meant evil against me; but God meant it for good, in order to bring it about as it is this day, to save many people alive." Through these pages, you will find healing, strength, and renewed hope—not only for yourself but for those you love. Enjoy!

—Mark and Nicki Pfeifer
NATIONAL CONVENERS OF USCAL
ICALEADERS.COM/UNITED-STATES

I applaud my big sister for having the courage to address the childhood abandonment that she, and her brothers faced growing up when our mother left us. Her 'Blue Jean Jacket' book shares the emotional struggles that she endured then and to some extent still carries, albeit with newfound knowledge and understanding to cope with them and to share her (our) story, and to be a light and inspiration for others who have also experienced childhood abandonment.

I mentioned to my sis that God knew what He was doing when He chose for her to be born first because of His omniscience and all-knowing that my sister would eventually be called upon to be the adult caregiver and quasi-mother for her four younger brothers while also serving as an aide to our father. While she might have thought it was a curse that she was born first, and then four brothers after her, I believe in God's ultimate wisdom that He knew that my big sister would be called upon, and with grace and love would rally to the challenge—and that just what she did, despite her own suffering of childhood abandonment. I will be forever grateful to her for what she selflessly did, and I shudder to think what would have happened if my eldest brother had been the firstborn and had been left with that responsibility; how things would have gone drastically different for me and my other brothers.

—Timothy A. Pirlo, M.Ed.
US ARMY RESERVE MAJOR (RET.), NASA RETIREE
EDUCATOR, LITTLE BROTHER

When our Lord and Savior Jesus Christ emerged from the wilderness to begin His ministry, one of the first things He declared was that He had been sent to heal the brokenhearted. He understood that abandonment, rejection, and deep emotional wounds often sit at the root of so many of our spiritual, mental, and even physical struggles.

In *The Blue Jean Jacket,* author Rena Perozich fearlessly addresses these core issues with both grace and truth. She gently peels back the layers of pain that so many carry silently—wounds from childhood, betrayal, and seasons of feeling unseen or unloved.

With biblical insight and compassionate wisdom, Rena exposes the lies we've believed and replaces them with God's truth. Her transparency and depth make this more than just a book—it's a healing journey. Each chapter serves as a mirror, a guide, and a companion, pointing readers back to the One who binds up the broken and sets captives free.

You will find your own story in these pages, and more importantly, you'll find hope. You'll discover how God can take even the most shattered places and redeem them for His glory.

This book is a beautiful invitation to let God heal what you've hidden, and it will guide you into wholeness, leading to a life of victory—free from the wounds and trauma of your past.

—Allyson Reneau

INTERNATIONAL SPACE CONSULTANT,
WORLD CHAMPIONSHIP GYMNASTICS COACH
MOTIVATIONAL & INSPIRATIONAL SPEAKER
ALLYSONRENEAU.COM

Writing an endorsement for what feels like a tell-all book is not an easy task. Being Dr Rena's daughter, I have seen what trauma can do firsthand and generationally. Just because it stopped with my mother does not mean the effect of it ends there as well. Like trauma being multigenerational, so can healing; hurt people may hurt people, but healed people bring healing to others as well. Let this book bring hope, healing, and truth as you or those you love go through the healing process of trauma.

—Jodi Perozich Phillips

OWNER OF RENA'S ORIGINALS
FACEBOOK: RENA'S ORIGINALS | INSTAGRAM: JODISCOOKIES4

This book is raw, real, and redemptive. With courageous vulnerability, the author shines a light on the often-overlooked wounds of childhood emotional neglect and abandonment. She invites us into the hidden pain of this, but she doesn't leave us there. Blending personal story with solid research and practical tools, *The Blue Jean Jacket* offers both insight and hope to anyone seeking healing. I've had the privilege of knowing the author for many years and watching her walk this journey firsthand. Her hard-won wisdom and authentic words will meet readers like a trusted friend, gently guiding them toward healing and hope as she encourages and equips them to pursue freedom and wholeness.

—Wendy K. Walters

VICE PRESIDENT OF ISM PUBLISHING
MOTIVATIONAL SPEAKER AND AUTHOR | WENDYKWALTERS.COM

CONTENTS

F O R E W O R D

"A good marriage is one which allows for
change and growth in the individuals
and in the way they express their love."

PEARL S. BUCK

I do not know if it is customary for a husband to write a foreword for his wife's book. However, I have been a first-hand observer of what childhood trauma can do to a person. I can testify that it affects every area of their life, impacting all their decisions, their health, wealth, and relationships ... and the list goes on. Only when it becomes painful enough will the search for truth begin, and with that comes the ability to heal.

Having witnessed this process across 48 years of marriage and walking beside my wife as she went through much emotional pain in her life, I can tell you that it wasn't until she began to press toward working it out with God and seeking professional help that she began to have the light come into the darkness. One day at a time, light kept illuminating the darkness. Because of my ignorance of the subject, I'm sad to say I was not always her best supporter. You don't know what you don't know, and what I didn't know made it more difficult for us both.

When you live with someone who has issues coming from trauma, the truth is that you are in need of some healing yourself. But my eyes were gradually opened as the transformation was happening for her. In the pages of this book, you will have a front-row seat to the journey of a woman willing to confront her trauma one step at a time to gain healing and freedom. These steps cannot be rushed through. Even the ones that sound simple take a great deal of focus and intention. Each step must be dealt with progressively. It may seem extremely long, but trust me when I tell you that it is the shortest route possible. Truly, the long way is the short way.

I won't pretend to have understood it all, especially in the beginning. As a man, my instinct was often to fix things or brush past the pain. But this wasn't something that could be fixed with logic or dismissed with time. Watching Rena do the hard, deep work of healing day after day has changed the way I see everything. It's opened my eyes to the strength it takes to face what most people bury. If you're holding this book, you're either on that road or you love someone who is. Either way, I hope you'll keep reading. What Rena has walked through has not only brought her freedom, but it has brought more healing to our marriage and greater effectiveness to our ministry than I ever expected. She's done the work. Now, she's handing you the map.

—Joseph Perozich

HUSBAND TO RENA PEROZICH
FOUNDER & CEO MFC MINISTRIES, INC.
CEO OF HOPERADIO.NET

THE BLUE JEAN JACKET

I N T R O D U C T I O N

Before my pen ever touched paper or my fingers touched the keys of my computer, I wrote these chapters—the ink was the tears upon my pillow each night. Over and over, I would capture my story as my tears soaked the pillowcase with the chapters you hold in your hand. The pictures I painted on these pages were in living color. Through the eyes of my heart, I could see the red of anger of being abused, violated, slighted, and wronged. I could see the blue of abandonment over and over again by those I loved and trusted. I could see the greens of envy and jealousy, thinking that if others got something, it meant I went without. Then, I would be overcome by the black of aloneness, trying to grasp for a direction to find my way out of loneliness, depression, and suicidal feelings.

I tried, once I was awake, to fill my world with contrasting colors. I'd strive to be the best, try the hardest, and make others the proudest, all the while feeling empty inside. If invited to the table of achievement I never felt I belonged. In fact, I never felt I belonged anywhere. I never felt good enough, whatever that was ...

I had this thing on the inside of me that was always secretly screaming, "Don't trust them. Don't trust her. He can't mean what he says. They lie. You're not safe." I thought everyone had those thoughts—until I didn't. I experienced an awakening in my soul that I had no idea had been asleep. It was a sort of survival coma that I had unknowingly allowed myself to fall into. The pain of awakening was more than I could stand. I cried a guttural cry that seemed to come up out of my inmost being. I was good at quieting this cry like so many times before, but this time—I didn't want to. I wanted it out. I wanted to cry. I wanted whatever was in there to come out.

Days turned into weeks, and weeks turned into months ... like they always do, but something was changing. I kept repeating the words I'd heard, "abandonment." It was a foreign word to me. I had never thought about or said the word "abandonment." I'd repeat over and over again what my coach had said to me, "I bet you're pretty clingy to your husband." I went into this cocoon to protect myself, but I had no idea what I was protecting myself from. "I'm guessing intimacy is difficult in your marriage." What right did this person have to delve into my personal life? Why did I have this knee-jerk response? Why did I feel like running? Why was I overwhelmed with emotion to the point of tears? I had more questions than I had answers. After the class ended and I was alone. I felt raw. I cried from that deep, deep place again. I didn't want anyone to know. It started wearing on me. I felt like there was this storm brewing, and I was afraid that, for the first time, I wouldn't be able to keep everything in control. What was happening to me?

The chapters that lie ahead of you are the storms unraveled, raw and real, which led me to my healing and deliverance. It was over a five-year process that Covid allowed me the time to slow down and invest in me for the first time in my life. I had never been still long enough or paid enough attention to how I was feeling. My life didn't allow for that. I didn't know people even allowed themselves to think about how they felt, what their memories were, or why

> I had never been still long enough or paid enough attention to how I was feeling.

they had huge spaces in their memories where they couldn't find years, events, people, and places. In *The Body Keeps The Score*, Bessel Van Der Kolk, M.D. writes:

> *The Trauma that started "out there" is now played out in the battlefield of their own bodies, usually without conscious connection between*

what happened back then and what is going on right now inside. The challenge is not so much learning to accept the terrible things that have happened but learning how to gain mastery over one's internal sensations and emotions. Sensing, naming, and identifying what is going on inside is the first step to recovery.[1]

If you can relate in any way, this book is for you. Abandonment affects your health, your wealth, and your relationships. In some form or another, abandonment is affecting you right now. That is why you picked up this book. Take my hand and allow me to help you walk through a healing process that will free your body from that pain that can't be diagnosed—yet you can't ignore it any longer. Let these pages help you understand why you're not making the money you know you are worth. It will give you clues as to why you seem to quit right before you succeed. It will help you answer questions like:

- Why am I such an overachiever?

- Why did I give others the card that reads, "Get Out of This Relationship With Me for Free" when they never even asked for one?

- Why do I procrastinate?

- Why do I have a hard time throwing things away?

- And probably most shocking, "Why do I attach emotion to inanimate objects?"

INTRODUCTION

There are answers. There is a way to overcome and heal from all the things abandonment has created in your life. The journey isn't a fast one. I won't pretend that the journey is an easy one. But I can tell you that I have made that journey, and I know the way. As a faithful guide, I will stay with you until the end. I will be right beside you on your quest for answers, understanding ... freedom.

ENDNOTE

1. Bessel, Van Der Kolk, *The Body Keeps The Score* (New York: Penguin Books, 2013, 68.

Healing meets us where
we are. Honors what's
been broken and walks
with us gently, honestly,
and without haste towards
integration, wholeness, well
being, and flourishing.

—Dr. Mark Chironna

The Epiphany

"Truth is always a turning point."

SHEILA WALSH

WHY I ATTACHED EMOTION TO AN INANIMATE OBJECT

Frantically trying to gather everything together to head out for a fourteen-hour drive, I kicked into panic mode. Oh, I'm used to rushing. No matter how hard I try, I seem to lack time management skills. When you raise yourself, you don't learn from someone modeling things for you—it is all trial and error. From an early age, I would ignore the clock and squeeze in as many things as I could from every waking moment. This pattern carried me through life. It served me in high school, sports, raising my four younger brothers, college, planning a wedding, and raising small children. It served me in co-founding a church with my husband, in writing my first two books, and even in finishing Bible college. Then, one day, it seemed that this pattern I had relied on for my entire life ceased to serve me and began to work against me.

I stood paralyzed, staring into my closet. Where was my *blue jean jacket*? I couldn't move. I completely shut down, panic rising. In *The Body Keeps The Score,* Dr. van der Kolk describes what took place in my body this way:

> *Trauma is expressed not only as fight or flight but also a shutting down and failing to engage in the present.*[1]

I can't go anywhere without my blue jean jacket. What would I wear with my classy black dress and strappy heels? My blue jean jacket. What would I throw on to signify my time to leave? My blue jean jacket. What would I cover up with if the car got chilly along the route of that long drive? My blue jean jacket. Without it, I might as well be naked! I run to the basement. Not in the washer. Not in the dryer. I run back upstairs and check the closet again. Breathing harder and starting to perspire, my hands are sweaty. I can feel my heart pounding in my chest. I raise my voice and shout to my husband, "Hey, have you seen my blue jean jacket?"

Gently, but firmly, he responds, "No, when did you wear it last?"

He knows me. Yelling back would only cause me to escalate. I try to think. My mind is swirling. *Did I leave it somewhere? I'll call the restaurant. Perhaps I left it on the back of the chair.* Dialing the numbers, someone answers, but I fail to even say hello. My manners are gone. "Did you find a blue jean jacket?" I blurt out.

Pause. A minute feels like an hour before the voice returns, and my heart stops for a moment, or am I holding my breath? "No one has turned in anything," the voice says.

My adrenaline surges, "Well," I attempt to sound calm, "may I leave my number in case someone turns it in?" I'm desperate. *Where is my blue jean jacket?* I call a friend. "Hey, have you seen my blue jean jacket?"

"I'm afraid not," she answers.

I am flustered, "Would you check your car, please? When did you last see me wearing it?" *She must know,* I think.

Time is ticking by. I have to leave. One of my "Steels"– that's my endearing name for some of the friends that I've had for over 40 years—had lost both her brother and mother in less than a week. *I've got to get to her. I need to be there to comfort her.* My mind races with guilt. She's always been there for me. I check my watch, calculating the drive—I *need* to leave. I continue looking for my blue jean jacket in all the places I have already looked numerous times. I know it. I feel it. But I can't stop it. I am going around in circles. *Where is my blue jean jacket? I can't go without it.*

Those around me are losing patience with me. They want to help, but they can't. I won't let them. *I need my blue jean jacket.* I can hear them talking, but I'm not there. I'm not listening. I'm remembering all the places my blue jean jacket and I have been. I'm now immersed in my own world. Panic has turned to terror, "What if it's gone?"

I didn't know it at the time, but I was experiencing *dissociation*, where my mind and body felt detached from the world as I fought to cope with trauma I wasn't even aware was there. Babette Rothschild enlightened me in her book when she said:

> *There is speculation that individuals who suffered early trauma and/or did not have the benefits of a healthy attachment may have limited capacity for regulating stress and making sense of traumatic experiences later in their lives. In some, it is possible reduced hippocampal activity, either because it was never fully developed (attachment deficit) or because it became suppressed (traumatic events), limits their ability to mediate stress (Gunnar & Barr, 1998). Under those circumstances, later traumatic experiences might be remembered by some only as highly charged emotions and body sensations. In others, it may be that survival mechanisms such as dissociation or freezing have become so habituated that more adaptive strategies either*

never develop or are eliminated from the survival repertoire.[2]

It's time to leave. My friend is in the driver's seat; my husband is wanting to say his goodbyes and pray for our safe journey. I can't be comforted. Both my friend and my husband are losing their patience with me. He speaks first, "Are you seriously that upset over *just* a blue jean jacket?"

I snap back, "It's not just a blue jean jacket. It's been with me everywhere I go. You don't understand."

Then, my friend pipes in, "We will get you a new one as soon as we get to St. Augustine." My heart sinks, and I am engulfed in unexplainable anxiety. I have to go ... *without* my jacket.

I feel bad about my behavior. Embarrassed. I'm sorry that I'm sulking like a petulant child. I want to suck it up and smile, like I always do. But I can't. For the next fourteen hours, I interrupt almost every conversation with a comment, a dream, or a might-happen miracle that would bring back my beloved jacket. *My husband could have found it in his car or at the church ... then he could overnight it to me. That could happen. Right?*

With each pit stop, I fumbled around. *Where's my phone? Where's my keys? Do I look okay? If I had my jacket, my phone would be in the inside pocket. My keys would be in the other pocket. Everything I needed would be in my jacket. But it's gone. It's not coming back. It's my fault. I've lost it. I won't be able to replace it.* The thoughts spin in never-ending scenarios, each one making me feel more and more crazy, more and more desperate.

I'm sure my friend was worried over my incessant ramblings about my blue jean jacket. She repeated the scenario over and over about me getting two blue jean jackets, two brand new ones. It didn't help. She just didn't understand. Once we arrived, the first place she pulled into was the beloved "Tar Jay," our fancy word for Target®. Excitedly, she showed me jacket after jacket. Too dark. Too light. No inside pocket. Finally, I settle for the Levi's® one. "Settle" being the key word. It at least had the inside pocket. It could hold my passport and the other inside pocket, my airline ticket. I wasn't sold on the silver buttons that read "Levi's." It wasn't MY blue jean jacket, but it would have to do.

We pulled out of the parking lot. My friend was thinking, "Problem solved. Now, she'll be quiet about that blue jean jacket!" Nope. I kept on. Following the GPS, we ended up right beside a Tanger Outlet. I decided to see if I could find the twin to my beloved blue jean jacket. I landed in the Aeropostale®, and I bought another blue jean jacket. I liked it better. It didn't scream someone else's name—Levi's®, Calvin Klein®, Old Navy®. This one just said nothing. It could be mine.

I wore that jacket with my classy little black dress and my strappy black sandals. My phone in one pocket (on silent, of course), and tissues in the other pocket. My hands were tucked in the outside pockets to keep me from appearing nervous or less than confident. I was going to be okay. My new blue jean jacket came through for me. In pictures, it hid my less-than-flattering mid-section. When someone, myself included, began to tear up—I was tissue-ready. This blue jean jacket was my new best friend. By the end of the trip, I was ready to return to "Tar Jay" and get my money back for that imposter blue jean jacket. But then my friend suggested, "Why don't you keep both? That way, if you ever lose one, you'll have a backup."

> ## This blue jean jacket was my new best friend.

Great idea. For the rest of the trip, I bonded with my new blue jean jacket. I still thought about my old one, but at least I wasn't obsessing over it. I wasn't constantly looping over and over in my mind: *Where, oh where, could my blue jean jacket be?*

Once home, I was thrilled to share with my husband about my new blue jean jacket. I shared about the funeral, the walk on the beach with my friend … and my blue jean jacket … again. "Oh, and did I mention I have two now?" Once I settled in, I began to unpack and put everything where it belonged: dirty laundry down the chute, toiletries back in the bathroom, luggage back to the guest room closet, and clothes never worn back into the closet. As I opened the closet door— there was my blue jean jacket! *How could I have missed it? Did someone put it there?* I held it in my hands. I brought it to my chest. I held it close enough to smell the combination of laundry detergent and my perfume. I held it as though it truly was my long-lost friend. I caught myself in the moment. *I'm treating this jacket as if it were a person. What's wrong with me? Am I crazy?*

Now, you may not believe in God or a higher power, but I heard, "The reason you're acting this way about your blue jean jacket is because of the **trauma of abandonment**. You assigned emotion to an inanimate object."

Inanimate? I think. *What does He mean I have assigned emotion to an inanimate object?* So, I look it up, "lifeless, spiritless."[3]

That landed. I had felt lifeless and spiritless most of my life.

Here I was again; the truth resounded in my very soul. The Voice was true. I had assigned emotion to my blue jean jacket. It was my friend. It was my source of comfort. It took care of me. I stood in my bedroom rehearsing all the places that blue jean jacket and I had traveled. We'd been to twenty countries together. Whenever everyone else was frantically looking for their airline ticket, "Old Blue" was faithful to keep mine safe for me, right there in the inside pocket. Once at the security gate, when everyone else was scrambling for their passports, I was calm. Old Blue had mine safe and secure inside its large inside pocket. I was taken care of.

Old Blue was making sure I had what I needed. My blue jean jacket had become "my someone." Once boarded on the plane beside someone I didn't know, Blue covered me up and stated loudly for me—since many times I couldn't find my own voice for fear of rejection—"Leave her alone … she doesn't want to talk to you." Then, later on the flights to wherever my assignment took me, Old Blue would be my pillow to rest my head on my tray table or cover my head to protect me from COVID. My blue jean jacket never failed me. Then the Voice of Truth spoke truth: I had assigned emotion to an inanimate object.

I loved my jacket.

So, where had it been? Why couldn't I find it? You may not believe me, but I know it doesn't matter. I may never know. I believe it was hiding in plain sight so I could discover a deeply hidden secret about me. I had an abandonment issue that had surfaced once again. Driving me, terrifying me, causing me to panic and hold my breath once more for fear of losing some*thing*—some*one* I loved. God was trying ever so gently to teach me that *things* can be replaced.

I was anthropomorphizing Old Blue, which means I was attributing human qualities to a non-human thing. For me, it was my blue jean jacket.

With this new-found revelation, my pendulum swung clear to the other side. Well, I thought, I will never do that again. Everything can be replaced. I'll just go get a new one; that will fix it. My mind was instantly racing again. My heart started to beat out of my chest, and my hands were soon dripping with sweat as I heard my inner conversation screaming with this recently discovered freedom, "Everything can be replaced. If someone doesn't like me and wants to leave me—fine—I'll just replace them!"

I ranted on until I'd almost exhausted myself without ever audibly speaking a word. When my internal rant was over, I heard ever so gently, "Easy girl, easy—let that pendulum swing back to center. We're not talking people here; we are talking *things*. There is a big difference." Spent emotionally, I slipped on my blue jean jacket and threw myself back into work—back into not feeling again.

I shut that chapter, but I would never forget the lesson. With every chance I was offered, I shared my epiphany. I was beginning my journey to healing. Little did I know I was just beginning to open the dark rooms of my abandoned soul and learn of my childhood neglect. I had never really understood what abandonment or childhood neglect was until I was working on my doctoral degree and read the book *The Emotionally Absent Mother* by Jasmin Lee Cori. She writes:

> *Not infrequently, survivors of childhood emotional neglect or emotional abuse minimize what they've gone through by saying something along the lines of, 'at least I wasn't beaten.' 'I don't have that much to complain about.' But a study reported by the American Psychological Association found that, 'Children who are emotionally abused and neglected face similar and sometimes worse mental health problems as children who are*

physically or sexually abused.' They discovered that children who have been psychologically abused suffered from anxiety, depression, low self-esteem, symptoms of post-traumatic stress and were suicidal at the same or a greater rate than children who were physically or sexually abused.[4]

Have you (or has someone you love) experienced childhood trauma? Suffered physical or emotional abandonment? Have you ever felt unexplained anxiety over something that seems too trivial to generate panic? Maybe you have also had an emotional attachment to an inanimate object or fixated on something so hard during a stressful situation that you, too, dissociated—and could not be present in the moment. If this resonates, I invite you to read on. As I share my story and the path to wholeness, I hope you will have a series of epiphanies that will spark your healing, too.

ENDNOTES

1. Bessel, van der Kolk, *The Body Keeps The Score* (New York: Penguin Books, 2013), 84.

2. Babette, Rothschild, *The Body Remembers* (New York: W. W. Norton & Company, 2000), 24.

3. Inanimate. (adj): 1. not animate; lifeless 2. spiritless; sluggish; dull. https://www.dictionary.com/browse/inanimate.

4. Jasmin, Cori, *The Emotionally Absent Mother* (New York: The Experiment, LLC, 2017), 109.

No One Likes You

"I'd like to make a motion that we face reality."

BOB NEWHART

We often judge people much like we judge the cover of a book. Sometimes, if we don't like what it looks like or the title is not catchy, we reject it. I thought people didn't like me—people who didn't even know me. Why? Because I never let people see me, at least not the real me. I figured if they knew me, they wouldn't like me. So, I became a performer. But the problem with being a performer and working so hard to please people is that you get tired of performing; that's why there are only so many performances before the show must end. Actors and actresses get tired, and it took a lot out of me to perform. I didn't know why, but many times, with those I loved most, I was so spent that I ended up giving them my worst. I understand why now, but then all I could do was get angry with myself for being so difficult with them. I learned long ago that my inner voice was not always telling me the truth. Erwin Raphael McManus said, "Our words create universes within the souls of those around us. When you speak, you are creating." I did not like what I was creating. I was repeating what had been modeled for me. I hated it. But I did not know how to change it.

But before I go further, allow me to give you some backstory. When I was between the age of innocence and grace, before becoming a woman, my mother left. My four younger brothers and I just came home from school one day like any other day— but it wasn't. There was no mom. That wasn't so different from other days because both my parents worked. We often came home before one or the other of them. On this particular day, however, when my brothers and I came through the door, the house was eerily quiet. You could feel it in the atmosphere that something was wrong. Then I spied a note on the table that read:

Dear Choppy,

I am gone. Rena is old enough to handle things, and all the boys are in school now. I will not be back.

Ginger

Her wedding rings were on the note. My young heart raced, wondering what I had done wrong to make her leave. Wondering what I could do to make her come back. Somehow, deep down, I knew she was gone for good. There was no one to explain what happened or why. There was no one to help us process even what it meant for her to disappear. There we were—five little kids left to figure it all out with our dad.

I don't know who said it, but this quote sums it up well: "The most painful goodbyes are the ones that are never said and never explained."

This horrible day is my earliest memory of abandonment, even though I never thought about it as being abandoned. I had no vocabulary to put into words what happened that day. I grew up in a silence I could not articulate. I don't remember asking Daddy where Mom was. I never asked if she'd come home. I simply functioned the best I knew how each day.

I embraced responsibilities far too heavy for my young shoulders, and almost overnight, the innocence of my childhood evaporated into tasks and chores and keeping everyone else afloat.

After Mom was gone, Daddy usually beat us home. I only remember this because mini-skirts were all the rage, and I was told not to wear a certain patchwork favorite short-short skirt … and I did anyway. I figured I'd make it home before Daddy and change. Nope. I got off the bus, and Daddy was waiting at the door. When he saw I'd worn that skirt to school, I swear steam came out of his ears. He asked me to go take it off and hand it to him. He put one foot on that skirt and then, with the other end in hand, tore it into two pieces, threw it at me, and said, "Don't think you'll be wearing that again." Needless to say, I didn't.

Dad was a gentle giant. Rarely, if ever, did Daddy get mad. When he did, I think he felt worse than we did. I only remember him punishing me once. He caught my brother and me arguing over dishes, picked us up by the back of the shirts, lifted us up off the ground, and banged us together. I laugh about it to this day. Our faces smashed up against one another with him shouting, "You two want to fight—fight!" Feet dangling and our little faces scrunched together, it must have been a sight.

My dysfunctional self served me well—raising four little boys, cleaning the house, doing laundry, helping my little brothers with their homework, and packing Daddy's bucket. If you don't know what a lunch bucket is, you probably didn't grow up in the hills of West Virginia, a coal mining town, or a limestone quarry. A lunch bucket had three parts. The bottom was filled with water, and the next piece fit on top and carried a fried egg sandwich or a pepperoni roll, and then the top had a piece of pie or some cookies.

When our Daddy came home, we would all run for the lunch bucket. We thought the water in the bottom was awesome. We'd fight over whatever was left, which was usually nothing. Oh, but once in a while, Daddy would surprise us, and inside the top part just above the water, we would find as many pieces of penny candy as he could fit in there. We would squeal with delight and run to show Mommy what Daddy had brought us. After Mommy left, that didn't happen much, or at least I don't remember it. Perhaps it was because there was no one to run to. Perhaps it was because he was too burdened to think of doing it anymore.

No one ever told me, "Wait till after dinner." No one ever said, "You need to go to bed." I realize now that is one of the many reasons I fail to calculate time, plan things past a day or two, or believe in a lifetime goal. As a child, a summer seemed like a lifetime. After Mom left, in the summer, I didn't have to worry about getting the boys ready for school or helping with their homework; I only had to be concerned with the house and making dinner.

All the things I did made Daddy happy—or at least relieved. It won me his approval and affirmation, so I became a performer and over-achiever. In my childhood mind, perhaps I thought that would bring Mom home or keep Daddy happy. I quickly filled up every moment. In her book *Hurt People Hurt People,* Sandra Willson writes:

> *It's as if we say to ourselves, "If I can just figure out how to be good enough (or smart enough, pretty enough, athletic enough, religious enough, slim enough, wealthy enough, sexual enough, unsexual enough), I can protect myself from being abused, unloved, abandoned."*[1]

I may not have had the cognitive processing or language to know that is what I was doing, but it is certainly at the core of why I worked so hard to keep up the performance. Band practice, basketball practice, cheerleading practice. My brother next to me did the same. He was a great baseball player. The next brother in line was a tinkerer. He would fix all our bicycles and keep our tires pumped. The next little brother was the only one who needed braces—on his teeth, his back, and his feet. Needless to say, I was very busy keeping all the plates spinning and organizing carpools and friends at school to help me get everyone where they needed to be.

During this time, we never heard a word from our mom. She never called. She never visited. Daddy was really sad. He had ulcers and would often get an upset stomach. I would learn much later how abandonment affects one's health as time went on—even my own health.

Once, before Mom left when we were really little, Daddy got really sick with bleeding ulcers. He was hospitalized for a long time in Martinsburg, West Virginia. Mommy put all five of us little kids in Daddy's pickup truck, which had a camper-type topper and a mattress in the back of the truck, and took us to see Daddy in the hospital. She came to a weigh station, and when she read the sign "All Trucks Must Pull Over," she followed those eighteen-wheelers right off the road. When the officer came over to the truck, he asked my mom if everything was okay. She said, "Yes, officer, everything is fine." He proceeded to ask her why she pulled over. "The sign said, 'All trucks must pull over.' I'm taking my five kids to see their dad in Martinsburg." He opened the back of that old truck and just told Momma she could keep on going.

We got to Martinsburg really late, so we were all asleep. Momma just locked us in, and early in the morning, there was a loud knock on the door. Momma got out of the truck and was told she would have to move along and find a suitable place to spend the night with her five children. All five feet of my mom stood up to that towering man and said, "Officer, with all due respect, these kids haven't seen their daddy in over a month, and I am not taking them anywhere until they see him!" Well, he parked beside Daddy's ole truck, and we all went back to sleep.

The next morning, we got to see our daddy. I have two memories of that day at the hospital. The first one was the beds. They seemed so high off the ground. They had steel bar headboards and were all on wheels. There were lots of men all in one big room—I've since learned it was a ward. I had to use a stool and be helped up onto Daddy's bed. I was determined to be reunited with my daddy. I hugged him hard. He needed a shave, and he didn't smell like his normal aftershave—Old Spice—but it was my daddy. I missed him badly, and I was so relieved to see him that I don't even remember my brothers being there. In my little mind, it was just me and my daddy caught in a moment of time.

> In my little mind, it was just me and my daddy caught in a moment of time.

The second memory is the black man in the bed beside Daddy. He told me he was going to get to go home that day, but he didn't have any shoes to wear. Shoes were important to me way back then. So, I asked Daddy, "Daddy, can you give him your shoes?"

Daddy didn't blink an eye. He said, "Do you want me to do that, sweetheart?"

"Yes, Daddy."

Looking back at the time of this writing, shoes were important to my father, too. He was one of nine children and didn't have shoes, underwear, t-shirts, or a toothbrush until he enlisted in the army. He always made sure there was at least a thumb's space between the end of our toes and the end of our shoes, or we couldn't have them. He always protected our feet and our backs. That was important to him. I remember him always saying, "You've got to have a good pair of shoes and a good mattress because you are on one or the other all day long." To this day, a mattress and, of course, shoes are very important to me. I know now what a huge sacrifice that was for my dad. I wonder what shoes, if any, Daddy wore home from the hospital. Dad was my hero. He was the most giving man I knew. His words still ring in my ears. Parents' words carry weight.

I don't remember leaving. I don't remember anything more about that day. I was already getting good at dissociating. I still didn't know how abandonment was affecting me, but I would find that out many years later.

Reality began to come quickly. Days turned into weeks, and weeks into months. Daddy would try to forget his heartache by going to the VFW. He would come home and be sick as a dog. Sometimes, he would even throw up. I never knew why until I grew up and learned it was from drinking. Daddy wasn't a drinker. In fact, I rarely, if ever, saw Daddy drink anything. Occasionally, he would have a lady friend visit, but they never spent the night or stuck around long. I think they knew Daddy was a package deal. If he went—he went with all five of us kids.

We all went to school, came home, got up, and did the same thing over and over again. No one at school really knew what was going on at home. If they did, no one said anything. Divorce was rare in those days, and for a woman to leave her five children was unheard of. Fathers may abandon the family, but a mother? I think the magnitude of that abandonment by my mother will affect me for my entire life. I will see a mug that says, "Momma Bear," and I will hurt. I was once told years ago that Hallmark gives cards to those who are incarcerated for both Mother's Day and Father's Day. They went on to share that all the Mother's Day cards are taken and often times even run out—but they always have Father's Day cards left over. That hit me hard. Even those who are incarcerated have a mother who loves them. A mother they want to remember. A mother who they know still cares about them. To this day, I still struggle to find the right card for my mom because they always say things like, "Through the years," or "All my life," or "You've been such a great example," and "For all the sacrifices you have made ..." None of them fit my situation. I can't lie. I refuse to be the Pretender or Performer. I want to be my authentic self.

Allow me to share with you some sobering information from an article entitled, "The Evolution of Divorce," published by *National Affairs*.

In 1969, the U.S. divorce rate was 3.2 per 1,000 population, with 639,000 divorces. Studies indicate that women in their twenties contributed over 60% to the divorce rate increase between 1960 and 1974. No-fault divorce law in California allowed unilateral divorce without proving fault, leading to a rise in divorces during the 1970s.

> *Since 1974, about 1 million children per year have seen their parents divorce—and children who are exposed to divorce are two to three times more likely than their peers in intact marriages to suffer from serious social or psychological pathologies. In their book* Growing Up with a Single Parent: What Hurts, What Helps, *sociologists Sara McLanahan and Gary Sandefur found that 31% of adolescents with divorced parents dropped out of high school, compared to 13% of children from intact families. They also concluded that 33% of adolescent girls whose parents divorced became teen mothers, compared to 11% of girls from continuously married families. And McLanahan and her colleagues have found that 11% of boys who come from divorced families end up spending*

time in prison before the age of 32, compared to 5% of boys who come from intact homes.

Research also indicates that remarriage is no salve for children wounded by divorce. Indeed, as sociologist Andrew Cherlin notes in his important new book, The Marriage-Go-Round, *"Children whose parents have remarried do not have higher levels of well-being than children in lone-parent families." The reason? Often, the establishment of a step-family results in yet another move for a child, requiring adjustment to a new caretaker and new step-siblings—all of which can be difficult for children, who tend to thrive on stability.*

The divorce revolution's collective consequences for children are striking. Taking into account both divorce and non-marital childbearing, sociologist Paul Amato estimates that if the United States enjoyed the same level of family stability today as it did in 1960, the nation would have 750,000 fewer children repeating grades, 1.2 million fewer school suspensions, approximately 500,000 fewer acts of teenage delinquency, about 600,000 fewer kids receiving therapy, and approximately 70,000 fewer suicide attempts every year.[2]

Once in a while, someone I didn't know would come to the house, and we would all be sent upstairs. We would listen through the register (a hole cut in the ceiling covered with a grate) so the heat could come up. But so did voices. Someone would say to Daddy, "Yes, we know you can take care of those four boys, but what about the girl? She needs a mom. She needs a mother." Little did I know that they were right, but Daddy would never agree—neither did I. It was evident Daddy was going to keep us together no matter what. I think Mom abandoning him was so agonizing that he would never do that to us.

It was evident Daddy was going to keep us together no matter what.

One day, while I was playing basketball at school, I started to bleed. I was scared. I thought I had played too hard. Maybe I was dying. No one else I ever knew had talked about bleeding. I tried to hide it with toilet paper. I felt terrible; then it got worse. It was hard to keep up with. I must have looked frightened and miserable because, finally, a teacher pulled me out of class and asked me if I was okay. By this time, I had learned to keep secrets. By this time, I was a performer. "Everything is fine," I said. I couldn't tell her. *What if she told Daddy?* I panicked. He was already sick from losing Mom; how could I tell him I was dying, too? *Both of us will be gone,* I thought. He was already throwing up sometimes, and he had started dating ladies. *Maybe I will get a new mom,* I thought, *then Daddy will be okay.*

Little did I know that the transition between grace and womanhood had come. I was not going to die; I just felt like it. Once I learned what was happening to me, I felt like a fool. Everyone knew about this transition but me. I was stupid. I was ugly. I was dumb. No wonder Mom left. She hated me. The voice of abandonment had raised its ugly head once again. I rehearsed my ignorance and reasoning that I was abandoned. I was not worthy of someone staying and walking me through the transitions of life. "Stay strong." "You have to do this on your own." "People will leave you, and you will have to figure things out on your own." "You are an embarrassment." Shame was starting to become my constant companion. In *Healing the Shame That Binds You*, John Bradshaw writes:

> *Shame-inducing thoughts tend to fall into three categories: self put-downs, catastrophic thoughts about one's inability to handle the future, and critical and shaming thoughts of remorse and regrets.*
>
> *Shaming thoughts about future sickness and catastrophe can make one chronically anxious. The "if only I hadn't done such and such" thoughts are sure ways to trigger shame spirals. And self-put-downs like "I'm too shy to make friends or get what I need," or "I'm so stupid," are ways to trigger shame spirals. Obsessions about your*

failures and limitations trigger spirals, resulting in severe depression. The more you obsess about something, the more intense the spiral. Thought-stopping seeks to stop the spiral at its source.[3]

One day, right before she left, I was being my naughty self and being hard to handle and disrespectful. Mom had a knife in her hand. She had been cutting up something from the garden, and I didn't want to work, clean, and do chores at that moment. I wanted to go do something with my friends. I was pushing her verbally to let me go, and she lost it. She just snapped. She pushed me up against the wall between the kitchen and dining room by the bar that separated the two rooms and pressed the knife to my throat. She said, "Go ahead, say one more word ... *one more word* ..." I could feel the blade of the knife pressing against the flesh at my throat. I knew she would do it. I believed her. The look in her eye was crazed ... and the next day was the day she left.

In my mind, her departure was my fault. I carried that guilt—secretly, silently—for a *very* long time.

But it was not my fault.

It is *never* a child's fault when a parent is selfish, cold, or irresponsible. But too many children believe that it is. Too many children absorb the weight of that guilt and carry it their whole lives.

Unbeknownst to me, all of this was the beginning of PTSD (Post-Traumatic Stress Disorder). The onset of it created by the abandonment trauma of a parent or caregiver who leaves a child at an early age, causing them to feel unsafe, unimportant, insecure, and unsure of how their needs will be met. This trauma affected me all of my life, and sometimes, I still catch myself in the loop, remembering and traveling the road of abandonment.

My mother was an alcoholic for years. As of this writing she has been alcohol free for over two years. Back then, no one outside the family knew; we didn't even know. We began to see it, and it was shameful. We knew it was terrible. We *knew* we had to keep it a secret. We learned early on to keep secrets. We learned it was important to look good on the outside, even if we were dying on the inside. In truth, our mother had abandoned us way before the day she left.

> *Alcoholic families are fertile seedbeds for shame. As the oldest child and "hero," I tried to fix the family and make my mother happy by being a good—no, make that the perfect—child. Naturally, I failed. Naturally, too, I blamed myself for not being good enough to do the impossible.*
>
> *In addition, my shame-bound mother looked to her children to mend her tattered self-concept. As a result, she conveyed to us that achievements which reflected well on her were what made us valuable. This early emphasis launched me into a life-time of perfectionistic performance and other*

people-pleasing behaviors to earn approval and love.[4]

How did I cope as an imperfect and hurting person who believed I should be perfect? I became a self-protective perfectionist, approval addict, clueless as to what was going on inside me. For shame that was binding me was also blinding me.

Sometimes, I still fear someone will leave me, and I am totally unaware of this fear, so when I am in doubt and feeling anxious, I jump to the worst-case scenario. I lack trust. Panic easily. Overreact and startle easily. *Why do I do this?* I wondered. *What is wrong with me?*

I would soon learn that trauma and ADHD often go hand-in-hand, and those who deal with this often find themselves lost in the middle. Until one day, we learn we are not so different from others. Lots of people have experienced abandonment at some level. A spouse left. An employer let them go. A parent rejected their child because of a gender disagreement. It's not that no one likes you. They just don't understand you. Or perhaps they are emotionally unaware

> **Trauma and ADHD often go hand-in-hand, and those who deal with this often find themselves lost in the middle.**

and immature—broken and dysfunctional, and they lack the skills to keep from projecting their pain in your direction. So they hurt you. But one day, you will heal. You will find your answers to the questions you didn't have the voice to ask. Until then, stay with me. Remember, I promised not to leave you on this journey.

There is a path through the pain to hope, healing, and wholeness. Let's keep going.

ENDNOTES

1. Sandra, Wilson, *Hurt People Hurt People* (Michigan: Discovery House Publishers, 2001), 63.

2. W. Bradford, Wilcox, (2009). "The Evolution of Divorce." *National Affairs,* 1, 81-94. Retrieved from http://www.nationalaffairs.com/publications/detail/ the-evolution-of-divorce on April 24, 2025.

3. John, Bradshaw, *Healing The Shame That Binds You* (Florida: Health Communications Inc.,2005), 209.

4. Sandra, Wilson, *Hurt People Hurt People* (Michigan: Discovery House Publishers, 2001), 63.

Sleepless Nights

"Child abuse (abandonment) casts
a shadow the length of a lifetime."

HERBERT WARD

Abandonment in childhood can have an adverse effect on sleep. Adults who fear abandonment are *more likely* to struggle to trust others and so often have difficulty falling asleep as well as staying asleep. All of our experiences, including how we were raised, combine to make us who we are, and how we react to stress, anxiety, and how we develop emotionally.

During much of my childhood, it seems we played outside from daylight to dark. I don't remember my parents being home very much. What I do remember is not being allowed in the house. I remember if I was thirsty, I would ignore it. If I had to go to the bathroom, I would hold it, and soon, the urge would pass. My most vivid memory is playing under the back porch. Whether we were told to play there or whether we chose to be sheltered from the sun—that is where we stayed. Our toys were the same regardless of our age or gender. We played with the old metal Tonka trucks. The earth was loose, black, and cool to my bare feet and hands, and we played under there for hours. Mom hadn't left yet, but she never came to check on us. Only when Daddy came home do I remember hearing our names called in order. "It's time to eat," he would shout. The routine was the same. Wash your hands, sit down, shut up, and eat everything on your plate whether you like it or not.

Afterwards, we all knew the drill. Clean up and do dishes, take a bath, lay your clothes out for school tomorrow, then go to sleep. That last part was easy because of how busy life kept us. I never knew Momma was training us to leave to us. Maybe she did not know either, but she certainly was preparing us so she could finally break free from what must have felt like a trap for her. She never laughed much. Rarely smiled. Never stooped down and made eye contact or cuddled or snuggled any of us. Just giving out instructions. Most of my memories of her are of her working, whether at a local restaurant, a resort, or at home; that is what she was always doing. I never felt like I was seen or heard. I longed for her to notice me. I longed for her approval and attention. When she was gone, I missed her. When she was at home, I still missed her. I craved more of her time and attention, and my little heart was convinced that it was my fault she didn't want to give me any. I must have done something wrong—I just didn't know what.

In *Adult Children With Emotionally Immature Parents*, Lindsay C. Gibson, Ph. D., writes:

> *Keep in mind that your thoughts about your parents are private. They may never know what you've gotten from this book, nor do they need to. The goal is for you to gain the self-confidence that comes from knowing the truth about (your) own story. You aren't betraying your parents by seeing them accurately. Thinking about them objectively can't hurt them. But it can help you … regardless of the severity of the parent's level of immaturity, but (the) net effect is the same: the children feel emotionally unseen and lonely. This erodes their children's sense of their own lovability and can lead to excessive caution about emotional intimacy with others.[1]*

Momma always looked beautiful. I remember sitting on my parents' bed, watching her get ready. How she put on her make up, teased her hair, and piled it atop her head, which made her look much taller than she was. I remember seeing beautiful bottles of perfume on her dresser, which I was forbidden to touch, though I never liked the smell anyway.

Chanel No. 5, I think that was her favorite. As I watched her get ready, I could tell she was happy—happy to be escaping the hard life of "five children before she was twenty-five," she used to say. It was as though she was proud of that fact, and still extremely thin and beautiful.

I would sit watching her and wonder if I would ever get to wear make up and be pretty, too. She never once allowed me to even touch her make up. When I grew up, I realized she no doubt had very little money to purchase the make up, and well, the perfume probably came from one of her many gentleman friends where she worked. I had no possible comprehension of this at the time, but years later, I learned Momma had never been faithful to Daddy. After 23andMe and Ancestry.com came to be, I discovered that at least one of my brothers did not belong to Daddy.

> Not knowing things about your family until later in life reinforces the ungodly belief that you're stupid.

Nevertheless, they are my brothers, and up until the day Daddy died, not one of us knew the difference. Not knowing things about your family until later in life reinforces the ungodly belief that you're stupid, that you're so naive. It proves what you have known all along—that you can't trust anyone.

UNGODLY BELIEFS

The best information I found on ungodly and godly beliefs was found in the book *Biblical Healing and Deliverance* by Chester and Betsy Kylstra. Keep in mind that there are hundreds if not thousands of ways to receive information that can be applied to your life that is productive, and healing for you. This book resonated with my spirit and the relationship I have with God. So, what are ungodly and godly beliefs, and when are they developed? The Kylstras define ungodly beliefs in this way:

> *[Ungodly beliefs are] all beliefs, decisions, attitudes, agreements, judgments, expectations, vows, and oaths that do not agree with God (His Word, His nature, and His character) and unfortunately, major areas of our belief system are usually made up of ungodly beliefs. Godly beliefs are all beliefs, decisions, attitudes, judgments, expectations, vows and oaths that do agree with God (His word, His nature, and His character). How do you know if it's a real godly belief, it is reflected in our actions. A real godly belief is rooted in our hearts, and finally, a real godly belief stands firm in the face of a challenge.*[2]

My entire childhood was a challenge.

As a child, I was the first one on the bus and the last one off. We lived in the country, so it wasn't unusual to have a long bus ride. I never questioned or thought it was strange that my bus driver would come in to visit Momma after I got off. I was just told to stay outside. Momma always locked the screen door. I never thought that was odd, either, until years later. Today, I wonder, *Did that really happen? Am I thinking too much? Not enough? Don't ask. Don't tell. Am I afraid to know the truth?* My ability to recognize my parents as emotionally immature was a painful discovery. In her book *Adult Children of Emotionally Immature Parents*, Dr. Susan Gibson writes:

> *A lack of emotional intimacy creates emotional loneliness in both children and adults. Attentive and reliable emotional relationships are the basis of a child's sense of security. Unfortunately, emotionally immature parents are usually too uncomfortable with closeness to give their children deep emotional connections they need. Parental neglect and rejection in childhood can adversely affect self-confidence and relationships in adulthood, as people repeat old, frustrating patterns and then blame themselves for not being happy. Even adult success doesn't completely erase the effects of parental disconnection earlier in life.*[3]

When my youngest baby brother was born, I told everyone he was my baby. Of course, everyone knew he wasn't, but I carried him on my hip everywhere I went. I would walk to the nearest neighbor's house (where we stole apples from her tree) and tell her about MY baby. I bathed him, changed him, and fed him. He was my real-life baby doll. Momma never seemed to mind. Never did she ask where we were, and the neighbors never said a word. I took on responsibilities that were way beyond my emotional level (EQ).

> *Children who had to become rough and handle things on their own may develop a rejecting attitude toward their own feelings. Perhaps they learned to keep distance from painful feelings they knew their emotionally immature parents couldn't help them with.*[4]

Today, I assume everything is my responsibility. I live in fixer mode. In her book *The Psychology of Intelligence,* developmental psychologist Jean Piaget shared through her observations that in order for people to learn anything new, their old mental pattern must break up and rework itself around the new, incoming knowledge. This process of internal breakdown and accommodation is key to continuing intellectual development.[5]

Cramming myself with knowledge and chasing every form of self-help, diagnosing myself and others, and enrolling in personal developmental classes I never used to finish was not helping me emotionally. I continued to live without emotional maturity because becoming mature meant facing painful memories and devastating shame, and worse yet, that ever-present feeling of abandonment. I wasn't well, and I couldn't sleep.

SLEEPLESS NIGHTS AND TROUBLED DREAMS

Traumatic stress (which can result from abandonment issues) is associated with higher rates of anxiety and depression. For many people with abandonment trauma, the fear of abandonment can be overwhelming. Anxiety can sometimes become so severe that it causes insomnia or nightmares. The anxiety and depression linked to previous abandonment can be overwhelming, interfering in several aspects of life.[6]

I am still unable to recall dates, and even timelines are muddled in my memory, but one night in my early childhood, after everyone was fast asleep, I heard a noise. I laid perfectly still. I held my breath. As the attic door opened ever so quietly, a man came out. He wasn't very tall. He had dark hair, and he approached my bed. All I remember is pretending I was asleep. I kept telling myself, "Don't move, don't breathe; maybe he will just disappear." As I am writing this, I am realizing that, to this day, I am still holding my breath. I catch myself doing that a lot. But now, I tell myself to breathe.

Years later, I remember seeing two men, seemingly my mother's friends. One of them asked me at a funeral, "You don't remember who I am, do you?" For some reason, a strong and bold voice rose up out of me, and with a look of anger from some deep recesses of my soul, I said, "Yes ... (long pause) ...I know exactly who you are." He backed away from me like he had seen a ghost. The color drained from his face, and he quickly disappeared. I have no idea where he went. It was just that face—that night—that man who stared down at me after he emerged from our attic.

Years later, I wondered if this man was also one of my mother's "friends." I wondered if his midnight attic exit was because Daddy came home early, and he would have ripped the man in two like my mini skirt. Had the man run to the attic to hide until everyone was asleep? I will never know. I will never ask.

But is it any wonder I don't sleep well?

I still have trouble falling asleep and staying asleep. I toss and turn and often awaken, startled from sleep for reasons that are still unknown to me. This has gotten better since I began to understand why and talk myself through it, but it is still difficult for me to sleep through the night soundly. Maybe what happened in your childhood has made this normal for you too. It certainly is normal for me. We aren't meant to have trouble sleeping—sleep is meant to be the most normal, natural thing we do without effort. But when you have childhood abandonment, it changes what is normal. And abandonment isn't the only cause of disrupted sleep; things like a sexual violation, other kinds of physical or emotional trauma, something like a fire or hurricane—something seen, heard, or perceived—can change what is "normal." It's okay. You are not broken. You are changed. There is hope. It will be hard work, but I promise that it will be worth the effort you put in to understand yourself and help others who love you to understand you too.

> When you have childhood abandonment, it changes what is normal.

After my mother left, I was plagued with nightmares. I was always falling, and I would wake up just before I hit the ground. The dreams grew in intensity, and I would wake up soaked with sweat, crying, and inconsolable. I would get out of bed, my little bare feet slapping the floor as I crept into Daddy's room and asked if I could hop into bed with him. He would always try to settle me and allow me to get in on what used to be Momma's side. After a while, I would fall back to sleep. To this day, I have to wear a night guard because I clench my teeth until I wake up with sore jaws or ringing in my ears.

It took a long time to figure all this out. I went to a dentist, then an orthodontist, and finally an ENT (ear, nose, and throat) doctor. My teeth were fine. I just had a lot of tension. I guess when you're a little girl and a man comes out of your attic, it might make you a bit tense. I had never told anyone. I never mentioned it to my mother or my daddy—or anyone else for that matter. I don't know whether I was afraid of the truth, or afraid of being called a liar, or perhaps being accused of something far worse.

THE STRUGGLE OF BROKEN TRUST

I sleep with both a mouth guard and earplugs, and my husband says I wake up if he moves. Poor man, he has never complained. I should add here that at this writing we have been married 48 years. I still have trust issues. I trust my husband in many ways, so it is hard to explain or articulate how abandonment issues affect our marriage. I don't know a lot about other people's marriages. But I will give you an example from ours.

I was given amoxicillin-clavulanate for a root canal procedure that needed to be performed. I had no idea I was deathly allergic to it. Right after I took the first dose, I got this anxious feeling, like I was scared. I could feel my heart racing and my hands started itching, then my feet and head. I thought maybe it might be a reaction, but I wasn't sure. So rather than call my husband and worry him, I just called my dentist. My dentist was with my husband. So, when he answered my call on his Apple Watch, of course my husband heard my voice. Not good.

I said, "Hey, Doc, I think I might be having a reaction to the antibiotics." In response to his questions, I shared my symptoms.

"Go straight to Med Express. This could be serious," he commanded.

"If you think it's necessary, I'll go, but I think I am fine," then I added, "Don't tell my husband; he will worry."

My husband had heard. He was worried. He was mad that I didn't want him to know. By the time I got to Med Express, I was in full-blown anaphylactic shock.

Why tell this story? Why bother to give the details? People who had to be on their own too early in life self-sabotage. I will address this in greater detail in the next chapter. For now, I just want to highlight how the things that happen in our childhood shape our trust and keep us locked in behavioral patterns that served us to survive then but sabotage our ability to relate to the world later in life. Dr. Gibson expounds on emotional immaturity:

> [Emotional maturity is] a real phenomenon that has been studied and written about for a long time. It undermines people's ability to deal with stress and to be emotionally intimate with others. Emotionally immature people often grew up in a family environment that curtailed their full emotional and intellectual development. As a result, they have an over-simplified approach to

life, narrowing situations down to fit their rigid coping skills. Having such a limited sense of self makes them egocentric and undermines their ability to be sensitive to other people's needs and feelings. Their reactive emotions, lack of objectivity, and fear of emotional intimacy can make close relationships difficult, especially when it comes to their children.[7]

I have been diagnosed with sleep apnea and sleep with a CPAP machine because my oxygen would drop to 75%, when the average normal for an adult is around 95%. I have a very detailed sleep routine. I have a certain pillowcase I prefer. I have a certain comforter I use. I have been prescribed sleep medication and even tried the teas, the melatonin, and the mushroom cocoas. I have a mouthguard. I look *really* beautiful—but at least I sleep. I have come a long way. Someone can even touch my arm or call my name, and I no longer "scream," experiencing yet another startle response.

I have always had vivid dreams. Many times, I will wake myself up living an event out. I have carried on conversations with people while being sound asleep, even while driving. I function as if I am awake, and only those closest to me figured this out. On a side note, they don't let me drive them around anymore. Now, I must admit these incidents are rare, but they tell you how severely trauma has affected me. I guess this would be like sleepwalking, only driving. Funny—Not funny. It is as though I am so driven to do what is expected of me that I can do it in my sleep. I am acutely aware of this danger, so I do not drive when I am overly tired. I do not push myself past my own capabilities. Whether this would be considered the risky behavior of ADHD or an abandonment trauma issue, I remain unsure. I am still researching this subject.

According to an article found on sleepfoundation.org, alertness and hyperarousal are the body's response to trauma. Because our brains develop so much during childhood, experiencing childhood trauma multiplies the impact on brain development. Dreams are often our subconscious mind's way of trying to process and work things out, so things that happened to us when we were very young—before we had abstract thinking, before we had developed awareness, and before we learned how to assign meaning to things, can get lost and jumbled in our subconscious mind. When we sleep, it emerges and often takes the form of a nightmare or deeply disturbing dream.

Up to one-half of children display some symptoms of PTSD after trauma. Psychologists call these Adverse Childhood Experiences (ACEs), and they have been found to increase the risk of mental and physical health problems later in life. Our brains do not know the difference between a real threat and the thought of a threat. So, when these nightmares occur, our body responds with real symptoms: the release of hormones, the muscles tense, the heart rate increases, and our breathing increases, preparing us for fight, flight, or freeze. Over time, this takes a significant toll on the body.

ACEs are linked to an increased risk of developing depression, anxiety, heart disease, and even premature death.[8]

These effects can last for up to 50 years, with each ACE increasing the risk of inadequate sleep as an adult by 20%. Thus, those with childhood trauma have more trouble falling asleep. Nightmares do not always cause you to wake up, so it is little wonder that those with more ACEs are twice as likely to feel tired after experiencing a full night's sleep. Sleep studies show that the more ACEs, the more disturbed sleep and severe insomnia are experienced as adults.

As I began reading books and articles on the subject, I began to realize I needed help. Suddenly jerking myself awake and gasping for air was not normal. Thrashing my legs while sleeping was not normal. I scheduled a sleep study, and it revealed that when I jerked myself awake, it was because my oxygen level was too low. My body was trying to survive. My body was literally waking itself up to keep itself alive. Once diagnosed with sleep apnea and put on a CPAP machine, my body no longer jerked itself awake. It did not help me fall asleep, but it did help me sleep without suddenly sitting up with my heart violently beating in my chest.

Sometimes, we just need to ask for help.

Sometimes, I just need to reach out for help. In my case, I needed medical attention. For you, it may be psychological help or spiritual help. This is often hard to do if you have experienced abandonment. After all, we think because we had to take care of ourselves then, we must keep taking care of ourselves now. This is simply not true.

According to Dr. Gibson, even if I continue with a victim reaction deeply ingrained, I can always reclaim my right to ask for help. Even more importantly, *I can keep asking for help as long as it is necessary.* Exercising agency—my decisions, responses, and actions to being a victim is the antidote to traumatic feelings of helplessness. I realize now how expansive the possibilities are in my current and future relationships.[9]

I have learned there is value in maintaining a regular sleep routine. I journal, read the Bible, and also study other books and articles that help me find a place of peace. I know that fighting sleep doesn't work. I have tried weighted blankets, and unfortunately, they cause me greater anxiety because I feel held down. I like a cool room because I can stay tightly covered up and not get overheated. I do not like to stay in my home or a hotel alone; I need to sleep where I feel safe. Whether it is from being raised with four siblings, the fear of being alone, or the fear of something happening to me while I am asleep, I am not sure. What I do know is facing the abandonment issue has opened an entire healing opportunity for me. I like me better. I have so much more peace. I have the words to express myself and even the grace and peace to do so. I am finally okay with being me.

ENDNOTES

1. Lindsay, Gibson, *Adult Children with Emotionally Immature Parents*, (Oakland: New Harbinger Publications, Inc.), 26.

2. Chester & Betsy, Kylstra, *Biblical Healing and Deliverance* (Grand Rapids: Chosen Books, 2005), 108. (Brackets and emphasis added).

3. Lindsay, Gibson, *Adult Children of Emotionally Immature Parents* (Oakland: New Harbinger Publications, Inc. 2015), 24.

4. Ibid, 114.

5. Jean, Piaget, *The Psychology of Intelligence* (Totown: Littlefield Adams, 1960).

6. "Understanding Abandonment Trauma" by Elizabeth Keohan, LCSW-C and clinically reviewed by Cynthia V. Catchings LCSW-S. © 2022 *Talkspace*. All Rights Reserved. Posted September 15, 2022. Retrieved from https://www.talkspace.com/blog/abandonment-trauma/#:~:text=Traumatic%20stress%20(which%20can%20result,in%20several%20aspects%20of%20life on March 1, 2025.

7. Lindsay, Gibson, *Adult Children with Emotionally Immature Parents,* (Oakland: New Harbinger Publications, Inc.), 47.

8. "Trauma and Sleep" by Rob Newsom, medically reviewed by Alex Dimitriu. © 2023 *Sleep Foundation*. Posted November 16, 2023 on https://www.sleepfoundation.org/mental-health/trauma-and-sleep#references-179912 and retrieved on March 1, 2025.

9. Lindsay, Gibson, *Adult Children with Emotionally Immature Parents,* (Oakland: New Harbinger Publications, Inc.), 171.

I promise that it will be worth the effort you put in to understand yourself and help others who love you to understand you too.

Self–Sabotaging Behaviors and Coping Skills

"One of the first steps in addressing self-sabotaging behaviors is identifying them."

JENNIFER CHAIN

LONGING TO BELONG

just shared with you about my sleepless nights. To bring that full circle, I need to take you back to when I was very young. Self-soothing behavior is part of healthy development in infants and small children. It helps them regulate their emotions. For children with abandonment issues, however, this self-soothing ramps up like it is on steroids! When caregivers give no cues for emotional regulation, children must find ways to cope with the stress. For them, it is less about regulation and more about survival. So, I learned early on how to self-soothe. I rub my index finger and thumb together on both hands—a repetitive motion. I never knew I did this until, as an adult, I drove my parents to the beach. Yes, I am talking about my daddy *and* my mother—yes, the same woman who abandoned me had now returned to take care of my aging father—but that's another story I will share with you in Chapter Nine) to the beach. I can tell you this: you learn a lot about a person trapped in a vehicle for fourteen hours!

> **You learn a lot about a person trapped in a vehicle for fourteen hours!**

I have a heavy foot, so I go about nine miles over the speed limit—always. When you raise yourself, you grow up with very few boundaries and usually don't keep the rules. You make the rules. Couple that with the risk-taking behaviors of ADHD, and sometimes it is the makings of a perfect storm. Speeding tickets. Accidents. Yes, that was then. Now, I have learned to manage time and leave myself enough travel time by calculating backward. If you know, you know. I also now allow others to drive—yes, I have learned I do not have to control everything. I can trust. Let others help. Trust others.

But, back to my story.

I was headed south to Daytona, my happy place. I was driving. Daddy kept braking, but it did him little good since there is no brake on the passenger side. I caught a glimpse of him rubbing his pointer finger and thumb together. "Daddy, do you always do that?"

"Do what?" he asked.

"Rub your pointer finger and thumb together?"

"I don't know. I guess I never thought about it, but now that you mention it, I guess I do."

"Me too!" I exclaimed.

I had been enlightened during this trip with my parents, especially with the way Daddy and I coped with anxiety, only to realize my four siblings had similar gestures and movements that they used to self-soothe, too. Movements, like rolling their eyes back and forth or tapping on the table with their hand, sometimes even moving the dinner table or moving other objects. Little did I know, this is actually a successful therapy that has helped thousands of military members and other individuals work through Post Traumatic Stress, anxiety, and trauma.

Dr. Francine Shapiro is the originator and developer of Eye Movement Desensitization and Reprocessing (EMDR). Dr. Shapiro, in her extensive research and clinical trials, noted when working with someone with trauma, when they began to share the experience, their eyes would begin moving back and forth, left to right, at a rapid pace. In her book *EMDR*,

The Breakthrough "Eye Movement" Therapy for Overcoming Anxiety, Stress, and Trauma, she explains the following:

> *It appears that within each of us, there is an information-processing system that is designed to process upsetting events so that we can maintain a state of mental health. When something unpleasant happens, we think about it, talk about it, and dream about it until it doesn't bother us anymore. At this stage, we can say it has arrived at an "adaptive resolution." We have learned whatever was useful about the experience (such as the danger of walking in dark alleys) and stored it in our brain with the appropriate emotion so it can guide us in the future. We have also discarded what is useless, such as the negative emotions, physical sensations, and self-belief that stemmed from the event.*
>
> *When something traumatic happens to us, however, this innate processing system can break down. Our perceptions of the terrible event (what we saw, heard, felt, and so on) may be stuck in our nervous system in the same form as when we experienced them. These unprocessed perceptions can be expressed as nightmares, flashbacks, and intrusive thoughts or PTSD. In EMDR, we ask the person to think of the traumatic event, and then*

*we stimulate the person's information-processing
system so that the traumatic experience can be
appropriately processed or "digested." As this
"digestion process" takes place, insights arise, the
needed associations are made, whatever is useful
is learned, and the appropriate emotions take
over.* [1]

AN UNSETTLING REVELATION

I remember the feeling of belonging. For a moment I basked in the pleasure of knowing Daddy and I were alike. As a grown woman, I experienced the exhilaration of knowing I was like my dad. Dad was *my* dad. Mom may have left, but Daddy stayed. That made him the hero, right? I certainly thought so … until after his death. Then, I realized I only made Daddy a hero because I made Mom a zero. I couldn't have both parents be a zero. Right? What would that make me? Also, a zero. A zero and a zero can only add up to a zero. So, Daddy, well, he would have to be the hero.

And he was my hero. He could do no wrong in my eyes, and I could never do enough for him. The ground he walked on was sacred to me, and being his little girl was a huge part of my identity.

After Daddy's death, which, by the way, I didn't think I would ever be able to survive, I realized a huge eye-opening truth. My mom left me once. Daddy left me over and over and over again. See, it was me and Daddy against all odds.

Me and Daddy taking care of my younger brothers. Me and Daddy holding everything together ... until Daddy would get a new girlfriend. Then she became the hero, and I became the zero. She would take all Daddy's attention. She would either stop by and cook and pack his bucket (or whatever) and then I wasn't needed. She was my replacement. She became the hero. I became the zero. Until ...

Until the new girlfriend wasn't around any longer. Then, the tables turned. I was needed again. Then, one day, Daddy got remarried, and my world fell apart. The lady he married was widowed with a young son and a daughter a few years younger than me. Both children hated us. I didn't blame them. Their daddy died in a mining explosion. My own mother's dad died when she was very young in a mining explosion, too.

Momma was the third child of four children. When her daddy died, he left behind a wife (my grandmother) and four children. If that's not bad enough, when she was pregnant with me, her mother (my grandmother) was murdered! The death certificate reads suicide, but that's the way it was back in the day. Secrets to cover secrets were made by those with more power and more money. My grandmother was locked in a barn, and the barn was set on fire. Perhaps that was the traumatic turning point in my own mother's life. The horrific event threw Mother into early labor. She was medicated and put in the hospital to keep me from being born too soon. So, even while I was in utero, my mother was detached, and her trauma came in between the natural mother/child relationship.

Daddy always told me he remembered bringing me home for the first time to our real home. When they left to take Momma to the hospital, the Christmas tree was set up. He remembered walking into the house in April, and every needle on the tree had fallen off and was lying dead on the floor. Up until that time, my mother had never held me. When Daddy had to clean up and throw away the tree, he handed me to Mother. I wish, at times, he would never have shared that story. Author Don Carter so distinctly writes in his book *Thawing Childhood Abandonment Issues*:

> *Children who get their dependency needs met fully on a regular basis will thrive, flourish, and grow at a healthy pace. Life will be good for these kids. In the worst-case scenario, kids who do not get their needs met at all will experience a failure to thrive, and many will die. Let us use the analogy of an emotional gas tank; if our needs are met fully, we feel full, complete, satisfied, content, and happy. If we don't get our needs met at all, we feel great emptiness inside. I have heard this emptiness described in*

> **"If our needs are met fully, we feel full, complete, satisfied, content, and happy. If we don't get our needs met at all, we feel great emptiness inside."**
>
> DON CARTER

65

many ways: a black hole, a void, a vacuum, an ache, or a longing. We may get our needs met half-way; we feel half-full, but something is missing, and we still feel an ache. These are emotional wounds, also known as original pain, and they result from an abandonment of our childhood dependency needs.[2]

I knew as an adult and because of the oral history of my childhood, which was told to me over and over again, that I was very unhealthy as an infant and young child.

COMMUNICATING AND CONNECTING

I want to take a few moments and focus on why we act the way we do. I realize there are no perfect families. Every family has "family secrets," but I just didn't feel attached. I did not have a sense of belonging as I grew up. I didn't fully grasp this concept until I read the book written by Dr. Tim Clinton and Dr. Gary Sibcy called *Attachments: Why You Love, Feel and Act the Way You Do.* The authors provide an in-depth and thorough explanation of the various attachment theories that occur during childhood development. The authors write:

Unlike many of God's creatures, a child is born into a world where it is utterly dependent on its mother for survival. It can't even keep itself warm, much less fed and comforted. We are discovering increasingly each day how dependent a child's developing brain is on its mother's sensitive, attuned, and responsive care. Our earliest relationships are profoundly important. They literally shape the chemical processes in the brain responsible for how we control our impulses, calm our strong emotions, and develop our memories of our early family life.[3]

Throughout my childhood, I knew that a mother was a child's first home. This only reinforced what I felt or didn't feel deep down inside my soul. I knew that babies and their mothers needed to bond right after birth. Taking a self-inventory of myself, perhaps this helped explain why I am not a cuddler, except now, decades later, with my grandchildren. Perhaps it plays a role in why I am not overly touchy with people. I lack compassion and empathy, many times unknowingly.

My love language is *not* touch. I feel awkward when someone hugs me. I hug others on my terms. In fact, left to myself, without the help of the Holy Spirit, all interaction would be on my own terms. Working on my emotional well-being, I have learned *The Five Love Languages*: words of affirmation, quality time, receiving gifts, acts of service, and physical touch, and I try very hard to speak the language most needed at the time. Discovering your own love language and the love languages of those you love is a necessity in life.[4]

I read *The Seven Frequencies of Communication: The Hidden Language of Communication* by Erwin Raphael McManus and learned about The Motivator, The Healer, The Challenger, The Commander, The Professor, The Seer, and The Maven. The book helps you understand knowing what communication frequency you are operating from. McManus writes:

> *Communication is the most intimate act between two human beings. Communication is the singular competency that transcends into every area of human development. Whether you are trying to connect with one person or millions, your ability to communicate will determine your ceiling.*[5]

Before I read this book, I did not know there were hidden languages of human connections. I took the assessment and found, not to my surprise, that I am a Motivator, Commander, and Healer, and in that order. I am sure that is one reason why, having experienced healing myself, I am sharing this cathartic work, *The Blue Jean Jacket,* with you right now. I understand not all of you were abandoned by your mother. But many of you reading this far may have been triggered and feel that you are beginning to understand that you have been affected or still are being affected by hurts, wounds, and bumps along this journey called life. As a Motivator, Commander, and Healer, I have included an extensive bibliography of therapeutic references at the back of this book. Use them. Share them. Check out the footnotes. Contact a specialist or counselor. Visit my website. It is never too late as long as there is breath in your lungs.

SELF-SABOTAGING PATTERNS OF THOUGHT AND BEHAVIOR

Like the story I shared about the trip to Med Express in the last chapter, I wanted help on my own terms. I didn't want a shot of Epinephrine. I wanted just a steroid shot. Why? Because they said that the Epinephrine could possibly cause me to go into cardiac arrest. "No, thank you." Being the persuasive firstborn, they listened to me. I started breathing again. I quit scratching myself so violently. I felt exhausted—like I had run a race, but I hadn't. My heart was still beating out of my chest, but I had things under control—until I didn't. The symptoms came back with a more ravaging violent force than before. I wanted to be in control. I tried to be in control. I couldn't. I wasn't.

The next best thing, then, was to find my husband. I *almost* trust him completely—which, in essence, means I should trust him; I try to trust him; I seem to be incapable of trusting him completely, but I am learning every day to trust more. I have implemented an annual practice in my life from reading books and articles by Jon Gordon, and that is to embrace ONE WORD for the year. And this year, as I really put energy into completing this book, my word is TRUST. But at this point, I draw the "Wait for my husband card." All women have these. Sorry, guys, keep reading because you've got a card too called, "Let me ask my wife." Which means you are scared she will kill you for buying that new truck. Right?

So there I was, telling the nurse I wanted to wait for my husband before they gave me the medication. "No, ma'am," she said with authority, "we cannot wait. This is a life-or-death situation, and you're running out of time." Reluctantly, I bent over and bared my cheek (and the shame). *Wow, does that stuff burn!* I might mention it also goes in slowly. Within seconds, I had relief. The injection went into effect, and my husband showed up on the scene. *I'm going to live to see another day,* I thought.

Did I mention this was all during COVID? Normally, you are admitted to the hospital for such a thing. But due to COVID, you were sent home with someone to watch you for 24 hours. Just when that was about to be the case, I experienced another wave of the dreaded allergic anaphylactic shock symptoms. This time, the firstborn, strong, untrusting, abandoned, emotionally-neglected child went in readily to whatever they wanted. There was no fight left in me, only dissociation. John Bradshaw, in his New York Times Best Seller, *Bradshaw on The Family,* addresses the practice of dissociation. He writes,

> *One major consequence is the disconnection between the act of victimization and the response to being victimized. Because the violation is so profound, the defense is equally profound. "Instant numbing" is my phrase for it. The technical word is dissociation. In dissociation, the violence is so intolerable that the victim leaves his or her body.*[6]

That is the way it is with abandonment and can be intensified with other disorders such as ADHD, anxiety, and depression. It's all or nothing. She loves me, or she doesn't. I'm good, or I'm terrible. Life is grand, or I think I will kill myself. There is rarely, if ever, a middle ground. Experience has told me all my life this is the truth. But this is a lie. I remind myself each day that there can be compromise, that there is a middle ground. There can be some good in a day, even if something bad happens. Just because the significant people in my life left me does not mean I am bad, nor does it mean that the world is not worth living in. But if you feel that way, I understand. I can help. Just stay with me. This pattern can change. The self-sabotaging behavior can stop, and you can relearn new ways of thinking and coping.

Just because the significant people in my life left me does not mean I am bad, nor does it mean the world is not worth living in.

Here is another great example—this one is procrastination. When you are on your own because a parent walked out, died, or just wasn't present physically or emotionally, even though they never went anywhere due to drug or alcohol or some other vice or addiction, you get to be your own boss. Since no one cares, you are in charge of yourself. Divorce happens, then who cares if you sleep all day? The kids are grown, and the house is empty; does it really matter if you eat dinner? If you don't want to do something today, who cares? If you don't do it right, who cares? If you work really hard to impress everyone else and win the race or get the "A," who really cares? No one—no one but you.

I didn't procrastinate about everything, just mostly my own goals, dreams, and desires. I had big dreams—big desires. I wanted to be an anchorwoman and tell the news on broadcast television. My daddy always said I had a great smile. He would watch the nightly news and remark about how pretty the newscasters were. He would look at me like only a daddy looks at his daughter and say, "You'd make a great newscaster. You're beautiful, and that smile will take you a long way. You can be anything." I believed him. I was young and impressionable. Life hadn't lied to me yet. I hadn't learned yet to pretend to be something other than what I was. I still believed.

Knowing our family wasn't rich, though no one ever told me, I figured college was out of my reach. But hey, I was a big dreamer, and Daddy thought I could be one, so I decided to work hard in school. Work was what I did well. It served me. Many times, it got me what I wanted. Hard work paid off. I got a full-ride scholarship to West Virginia University—WVU. I majored in journalism. I loved all my classes, except the basic required classes, but I sucked it up. I knew by then how to do that. Be what the professor was looking for. Be present. Never miss a class. Raise your hand. Ask questions. Pretend to be interested. Life has a way of training you with trauma. I have since learned trauma may have trained me, but I now use the training for reigning, not whining. I can overcome all odds and so can you! Even when your traumatized soul makes a wrong decision for fear of someone leaving—yet again, you can pick yourself up and use what knocked you down to help others get back up, too.

So, college was humming along. My professors loved my writing and my public speaking assignments. I was like an otter in the zoo. Applaud me, and I will do even better. I did all the normal things one does in college—well, that is, if you've grown up too fast and learned to be an adult way too early. Author Don Carter, in his book *Thawing Childhood Abandonment Issues,* writes the following:

> *When the first child comes along, he or she finds out fairly quickly that in order to get any time, attention, affection, and direction in the family, he or she has to do something outstanding to get noticed. So, this child usually becomes the Hero. There are two kinds of family heroes. The first is the flashy hero: aka the Responsible One or the Parentified Child. This child who comes home from school early every day, does the laundry, gets the mail, prepares dinner, does the dishes, takes care of the younger kids and, in essence, becomes a parent at ten years old.[7]*

I went to college at eight in the morning until noon. Then, I would work my college work-study assigned job until 4:00 p.m. Then, I would go to the mall and work until 9:00 p.m. Every day was the same. With one year left to go, I met my husband-to-be. He told me he didn't want to be married to a news reporter traveling the world with a briefcase. My exact dream ... but I was afraid of being abandoned again. I was terrified of someone else walking out of my life. So, I did what normal abandoned, emotionally-neglected people do. I did the impulsive, risky behavior chosen by my dopamine-searching ADHD brain: I changed my major. And when his job took us out of state, I lost my scholarships, too.

> I was terrified of someone else walking out of my life.

Admittedly, years into our marriage, I resented him for that. Why couldn't he have encouraged me? Why couldn't he have sacrificed for my dream? Why was this not a conversation? Why, you ask? Because that's not how it went down the day I came home to that letter from my mother to my father. No discussion. No compromise. No, "Could we maybe try this?" No ... nothing. Just a "suck it up and do what it takes." I had no grid for having that conversation. Today, I *am* a news reporter. I carry the good news of Jesus Christ. I travel around the world with a briefcase. I love my job. My husband encourages me. Right now, I am writing this while sitting in the sunshine in one of my favorite places in all the world.

SHIFTING FROM SELF-SABOTAGE TO WHAT SERVES ME

It took me years of sabotaging myself and allowing others to control me to realize I needed help. Today, I don't ignore my appetite or my bodily functions. I don't give up on myself or my dreams for fear that others may abandon me. I have learned I am creative. I am spontaneous. I am adventuresome. I have all the great traits of ADHD, as well as some of the challenges. I am loveable. I mean, you bought my book—you think I'm valuable. Okay, maybe the pendulum swung too far again—but then again, maybe not. Life means we take the good with the bad. There are valleys. But there are also some awesome views on the mountaintop that many never get to see. We do.

Time management has been a huge issue with me. I try to get way too much done in the mornings and not being a morning person leads to spills and crashes. I can't tell you how many compacts and eye shadow palettes have shattered on the floor in my wake of trying to get ready. The self-induced pressure leads to hurriedly packing things for the day and tidying things up for my peaceful arrival back home. This never works because I can't remember when I tidied up where I put everything. I habitually, well most of the time, well more times than not, okay, I'm late before my day ever gets started. My anxiety is a 10, and it's only 9:00 a.m. I will call a friend to talk me off the ledge, and she will yell at me and say, "You never account for driving time!" So, I will hang up on her and call my husband and start the conversation off with, "You're never gonna believe this ..." Of course, he does, and so does she. They know me well, but remember, I am a work in progress. I am learning to shift my behaviors from self-sabotaging ones to finding ways to incorporate habits that better serve me. From the beginning of this book until now, I find that I am often a half-hour early. I set timers. I set reminders. I know I have a high IQ and that I am a very capable adult. I work with myself. I have upped my self-awareness, and I understand myself and treat myself with love and care. You can learn this, too.

Often, when I am at the point of exasperation, I recognize the need to have a close friend talk me through everything I did get done in a day. My counselors have encouraged me to write things down when I do them and cross them off my long "To Do" list. My perfectionism drive is never satisfied. I can never get all I want done, done in a day. Things always take longer than I account for. But knowing this and learning this is the way my brain operates somehow made it better for me. I work with myself now, not against myself. I refuse to compare myself. I take care of my body, my soul, and my spirit. I have daily affirmation statements I use. I take time to do what I refer to as "Daily Devotions," which include, but are not limited to, reading portions of scripture and books broken into daily snippets of loving, motivating, or informational readings, podcasts, TedTalks, Audible books, and whatever else I can get my hands on.

> I work *with* myself now, not *against* myself.

As a child, my "To Do" list left for me by my parents (spoken or unspoken, implied or assumed) was always longer than my age-appropriate abilities could handle. I was defeated before I started. This pattern has followed me into adulthood. Today, I am the parent making the list myself. Old habits have been hard to break. On a positive note, people compliment me on how fast I can make a meal or transition from task to task. It's interesting the things that harm and hurt us, can also serve to help us. The ability to handle pressure serves me well even to this day. Some things I have decided to just be grateful for.

Rather than self-sabotaging, I have learned that when you are not taught at an early age to manage yourself, you either must be managed later in life, which is often times embarrassing and reinforces ungodly beliefs about oneself, or you learn to do the self-work and teach yourself. Read the books, get the help you need, and yes, sometimes take the medication, if necessary, even if for just a short period of time until you are capable of using healthy coping skills and facing life head-on with the knowledge that our Daddy God believes we can do or be anything. The world has lied to us. We have lied to ourselves. Others have lied to us. However, we can accept the truth. The truth is always better than the best lie. The truth really can set us free.

> **The truth is always better than the best lie. The truth really can set us free.**

ENDNOTES

1. Francine, Shapiro & Margot Silk Forrest, *EMDR Eye Movement Desensitization & Reprocessing,* (New York: Basis Books, A Member of the Perseus Books Group, 1997), 28-29.

2. Don, Carter, *Thawing Childhood Abandonment Issues,* (www.internet-of-the-Mind.com, 1995). 18-19.

3. Tim, Clinton & Gary, Sibcy, *Attachments,* (Brentwood: Integrity Publishers, 2002),

4. Gary, Chapman, *The Five Love Languages,* (Chicago: Northfield Publishing, 2004), 133.

5. Ervin, McManus, *Seven Frequencies of Communication,* (New York: The Arena Publishing, a division of The Arena Community, LLC, 2024), 28.

6. John, Bradshaw, *Bradshaw On: The Family: A New Way of Creating Solid Self-Esteem, (*Deerfield Beach: Health Communications, Inc., 1996), 129.

7. Don, Carter, *Thawing Childhood Abandonment Issues,* (www.internet-of-the-Mind.com, 1995). 33.

C H A P T E R   F I V E

Ignoring Appetites and Bodily Functions

"People think healing looks like having huge visible breakthroughs when, really, it's just a series of small decisions that reprogram your subconscious mind. One healthy activity at a time is a great starting point."

UNKNOWN

Even before Momma left, we were left. We were left alone. We were left with sitters. We were left at Grandma's. When you are left a lot—well, you feel left. Alone. On your own. Vulnerable. Unsafe. You can miss some important life lessons, and you learn to ignore a lot.

Remember when I shared with you about playing under the porch with Tonka trucks? Those childhood days of ignoring appetites and bodily functions began at an early age for me. In my earliest memories, I can still smell the dampness of the ground under our old porch. I can still feel the cool, loose earth beneath my feet. It was a welcome place from the hot sun, as we were told to go outside and play even on the hottest days during summer break. I can remember how I would scoop that dark, crumbling earth into nice, neat piles for my brother to move with his truck. I promised this book would be real and raw, remember? Well, this chapter is just that, real and raw. As I am remembering and sharing my past with you, I want you to remember your past, too. In order to heal, you need to understand the trauma of abandonment—to see it. Feel it. Smell it. Deeply sense it. Let yourself go back there.

I remember the urgency of needing to go to the restroom. My little brothers could just go to the edge of our property surrounded by woods and let it go. Not me. I'm a girl, which was just one more reason why I wanted to be a boy. It seemed that boys *always* had another set of rules to play by.

So, being a girl and not being allowed to go into the house, I ignored having to go to the bathroom. I learned to hold it. I can still hold it an entire day, not something I am proud of. If you suffer from or battle with the disability of ADHD, this is not abnormal. So, adding abandonment to the mix, it's easy to understand why I now fight bladder issues. I truly try to remember to go to the restroom, but then I lose focus and forget. I am learning not to be so hard on myself. It's just never been about me, so it's hard to recognize when I just need to take care of myself. It's foreign to me when others say, "Excuse me, I'm going to the restroom," or "I should go before we leave ... before the drive, before the dinner, before ..." *Great idea!* I hear my inner self say. So, then I go too. But nope, it is not naturally in my vocabulary.

As a child, no one ever asked me, "Do you need to go to the bathroom?" I am still somewhat embarrassed that, as an adult, I do not have these thoughts on my own. As a matter of fact, as a grown adult, when I heard a lady say those words, I thought to myself, *Wow, that's a fantastic idea. I should do that, too. I should do that all the time.* It helped a great deal for me to realize this was part of developing emotional maturity I had missed. I began to feel like I was on some catch-up plan. I was in control and taking care of myself. *Good job, self!* I'd been given a key to open a door that I didn't even realize I had locked from the inside.

> I'd been given a key to open a door that I didn't even realize I had locked from the inside.

I began to take steps to unlock myself from that door during the two-year process of obtaining my doctorate and reading everything I could on childhood trauma, specifically abandonment. To my surprise, I had a difficult time finding books or journal articles on the subject of abandonment. There were plenty of books on Childhood Emotional Neglect (CEN), Trauma, and PTSD, but not specifically on abandonment. Abandonment was a way of life for me. I never knew it, but once I did, it had a snowball effect on everything.

Pieces of my life's puzzle started swirling around in my head as I frantically grabbed one piece and put it in place. I read more than 40 books and researched several articles in an effort to better understand myself and find out why I act the way I do. With each book, with each new piece of knowledge, I felt lighter. I cried a lot. I must admit I hurt deeply. I think back and realize I grieved a childhood that no one realized I missed, not even me. My parents, as far as I was concerned, were great. Small, wonderful memories like Christmas or camping were all I remembered. There were a few little things, like my mother brushing my hair once with her hand while I laid my head on her lap in the car while Daddy was driving. I had just never seen myself as abandoned.

Maybe I was protecting my already wounded soul? Maybe all my attempts to be worthy and valuable had kept me moving so fast I had never slowed down long enough to listen to the still, small cry in the deep recesses of my heart. I don't know because once I saw it, I couldn't fathom how I had not seen it all along. It was as obvious as the nose on my face.

In reading Dr. van der Kolk's *The Body Keeps the Score,* I found the medical and psychological language to describe what was going on in my mind, body, and spirit. He writes:

> *... the most important job of the brain is to ensure our survival, even under the most miserable conditions. The brain is built from the bottom up.*

It develops level by level within every child in the womb, just as it did in the course of evolution.[1]

I must stop here and politely disagree with Dr. van der Kolk in that I am a firm believer in God and that He created all living things. Nevertheless, I have several more important details from this book that have brought revelation to what has transpired throughout my life. I have my doctorate in Strategic Leadership. Dr. van der Kolk is a medically trained psychiatrist and researcher. So, without pausing to correct his theology, let me share what he writes in his book that will bring everything together regarding the body and how trauma and abandonment can affect it.

The most primitive part, the part that is already online when we are born, is the ancient animal brain, often called the reptilian brain. It is located in the brain stem, just about the place where our spinal cord enters the skull. The reptilian brain is responsible for all the things that newborn babies can do: eat, sleep, wake, cry, breathe, feel temperature, hunger, wetness, and pain: and rid the body of toxins by urinating and defecating. The brain stem and the hypothalamus (which sits directly above it) together control the energy levels of the body. They coordinate the functioning of the heart and lungs and also the endocrine and immune systems, ensuring that these basic life-sustaining systems are maintained with the relatively stable internal balance known as homeostasis. Breathing, eating, sleeping, pooping, and peeing are so fundamental that their significance is easily neglected when we're considering the complexities of mind and behavior. However, if your sleep is disturbed or your bowels don't work, or if you always feel hungry or if being touched makes you want to scream (as is often the case with traumatized children and adults), the entire organism is thrown into disequilibrium.

It is amazing how many psychological problems involve difficulties with sleep, appetite, touch, digestion and arousal. Any effective treatment for trauma must address these basic housekeeping functions of the body. Right above the reptilian brain is the limbic system. It's also known as the mammalian brain, because all animals that live in groups and nurture their young possess one. It is the seat of the emotions, the monitor of danger, the judge of what is pleasurable or scary, the arbiter of what is or is not important for survival purposes. It is also a central command post for coping with the challenges of living within our complex social networks. The limbic system is shaped in response to experiences, in partnership with the infant's own genetic makeup and inborn temperament. Another way of describing neuroplasticity, the relatively recent discovery that neurons that "fire together, wire together." When a circuit fires repeatedly, it can become the default setting--- the response is exploration, play and cooperation; if you are frightened and unwanted, it specializes in managing feelings of fear and abandonment.[2]

Dr. van der Kolk continues with a description and explanation of the reptilian brain and limbic system known as the "emotional brain." Throughout the book, he explains that the emotional brain is at the heart of our central nervous system and that its key task is to look out for your welfare. If it detects danger or a special opportunity—such as a promising partner—it alerts you by releasing a squirt of hormones. The resulting visceral sensations (ranging from mild queasiness to the grip of panic in your chest) will interfere with whatever your mind is currently focused on and get you moving-- physically and mentally in a different direction. Sound familiar to you? Oh, shiny! (Did I mention I love Dory in the movie *Finding Nemo*? I totally relate, as I can lose focus easily and then hyper-focus on the distraction that just totally took me off the task I was working on!)

Just as no one ever asked me if I needed to use the restroom, no one ever asked me, "Are you hungry?" My mother was always thin, and I only remember her drinking coffee and eating one meal a day--dinner. I'm not as small-boned as my mother, and I am at least four inches taller. I am built like an athlete, with broad shoulders and legs that are sculpted like a statue. I have even been wrongly accused of having calf-muscle implants. *Is that even a thing?* Anyway, for some reason, I always thought I was fat. I have no waist and, well, no cushion on the backside either. I learned early on that I was not perfect. Only this time, I could do nothing to change it. I would have to accept the genes I'd been given. I never liked my body growing up, and I still struggle with self-image.

I got too much attention at a young age because I developed sooner than others my age. I skipped the training attire and went straight to the minimizers. But I must admit my body has carried three children and served me well for almost 70 years. I am grateful. If we begin to practice gratefulness, we often forget to complain.

> ## If we begin to practice gratefulness, we often forget to complain.

My brothers were lean and muscular. Their stomachs never stuck out, and of course, they had no chest. Me? I was "well-blessed," as some would say, in that category. Comments were often made about how "chesty" I was. Or worse, my thin mother would say, "You'll get fat eating that. That won't look good on your hips." Her comments were hurtful. I don't think she meant harm. I truly believe she wanted a pretty, thin, and petite daughter like herself. But I wasn't her.

I look much more like my father, the Italian side of our family. I have long, straight, fine, light brown to blonde hair like Daddy. Mother always gave me a perm to make me look like Shirley Temple (you Gen Z and Millennials may have to Google her). Mother has very dark, dancing eyes. I have eyes like my grandpa—the only grandpa I ever knew. My uncle always called them "special eyes." That made me feel better. But it did not fix that comparison disease that I would never be pretty enough. American author and motivational speaker Jack Canfield once said, "I generally find that comparison is the fast track to unhappiness." Well, I would agree with Jack. Abandonment caused me to be very unhappy.

My brother was always called "pretty boy" by my grandma (the only grandmother I ever knew) because of his big blue eyes. Oh, how I wanted big blue eyes. He also tanned easily, and Mother loved the sun. His blond hair would lighten up in the summer, and he looked like a Coppertone baby. Oh, to be a boy …

It seemed that no matter what the boys ate, everyone would comment on how skinny they were. I, on the other hand, was never referred to as skinny until I started starving myself as a young adult and even into my forties. I battled seeing myself as fat. I started running after my third child. It took the weight off quickly and got me quite a few trophies. Oh, how we abandoned, neglected adult children need those trophies and accolades. I started aerobics. Then, I decided I wanted to teach aerobics. So, I studied and got ACE certified (American Council on Exercise).

I would teach several classes a day, but good was never good enough. I always had to be the best. I always had to win. Be number one. I was trying to satisfy a need, to fill a hole that could never be satisfied with a title, trophy, a ribbon, or a plaque on the wall. I was looking for acceptance from being abandoned. I also needed that dopamine hit for my ADHD brain to want to live. I finally had this epiphany. I even thought of a label for it: "Acceptance Hunger." That's it—I was hungry for acceptance. Food couldn't fill it. Though I often tried to silence the greedy voice of need. Once, I ate an entire box of Peanut Butter Captain Crunch® cereal because I knew when my four little brothers came home and started eating it, there wouldn't be enough for me. Did I mention I threw up? To this day, I can't even look at the box without feeling queasy.

Abandonment had reared its ugly head once again. There would never be enough for me because that's what your trauma tells you. You buy too much. You wear too much makeup. You try too hard to make friends. But it is a lie. You are enough. I am enough. Just because I have learned to ignore my appetites and my bodily functions does not mean I can no longer ignore my feelings. So today, I am learning to listen to my body. I allow myself to notice how I feel. I eat when I am hungry (if I remember), and I set timers to remind me to drink water. I matter. One day you will have the opportunity to deal with your past rather than it dealing with you. Maybe today is that day. This book can help. Keep reading—you've got this!

Whoever, whenever, whatever happened to you and me, we are survivors.

We can face the hard things.

We can learn to tune into our body and listen to what it needs.

We can meet those needs in a healthy way—and then, maybe, just maybe, we can help others.

When I began this journey, all I could hear inside my head was I was never enough. I would never be enough. There was not enough of a mother's love for me—that's why she left. There was never enough love from Daddy, which is why he always chose the boys over me or replaced me with a girlfriend after Mother left. I knew I was a disappointment from the start. After all, Italians are supposed to have boys. The firstborn should be a son. My heart would scream, but nothing ever came out of my mouth. I had shut down. I had silenced my voice. No, I had lost my voice.

I began to tune into the voice of abandonment ... until ...

Until the day I took that class. I am forever grateful for the questions I was asked. I may have never asked myself those questions. Those questions led me to the answers I desperately needed; I just couldn't see it. There is never a reason to slap a blind man and tell them to look. They can't. They are blind.

I was blind.

Mother used to tell the story that when she had me, she never got any flowers from Daddy. When my brother was born, she got two vases full, and one even had boxing gloves attached. *Why did she have to tell me that story?* I felt like a disappointment. I was quicker and faster than my brother. I was almost four years older than him. But, when Dad would throw a football and yell, "Run out for the pass," I would run and out catch that ball every time. Daddy would just say, "Let your brother catch this one." Then, when he did, that's all we heard about at the dinner table—what a good catch my brother made. I understand now; I mean, after all, I wasn't going to play football in school or play professional ball for a living. But maybe one of my brothers would. So, my inner voice began to tell me to give up, that it didn't matter. Quit trying. This has caused me to often see a task or project bigger than it is, and so I procrastinate even getting started. I tell myself it won't work. I could never do that. It doesn't matter. Part of that I realize now is also the ADHD that had gone undiagnosed until much later in my life. One day, I just couldn't keep all the plates spinning anymore. I just started dropping them. As they shattered on the floor, my anxiety took control. I was broken, and I needed help.

Sometimes, I would go into a freeze mode—I became embolized. I just wanted to sleep. I didn't want to see anyone. I would deny that I dealt with depression. I had no idea there was such a thing as ADHD paralysis, which, according to ADHDAdvisor.org, is the inability to think or function effectively when overwhelmed by one's environment or needing to deal with a surplus of incoming information. I got so overwhelmed with finishing this book that it took me over five years. The thought of meeting deadlines, having everything perfect, and making decisions about what to share and how to organize my thoughts put me into repeated paralysis. I didn't want to hurt anyone. *What would Mother think? My brothers? My husband? Friends?* I was stuck. COVID hit, and my world changed like so many others, but this time, I could not adapt and overcome. I could not control my world.

With abandonment and trauma already stirring in my body, it is now easier for me to understand and accept my behavior. I was not being lazy. I was procrastinating. I was in a freeze mode. Dr. van der Kolk helped me to understand, in part, what was happening to me when he wrote:

> *When something reminds traumatized people of the past, their right brain reacts as if the traumatic event were happening in the present. But because their left brain is not working well, they may not be aware that they are reexperiencing and reenacting the past—they are just furious, terrified, enraged, ashamed, or frozen.*[3]

Memories kept flooding in. It was dinner time. When Mom yelled dinner, we ran. It's the only meal I remember except for a cup of cocoa wheats before heading for school. Oh, and I will never forget those great school lunches when everything used to be homemade by the lunch ladies. I think those cooks treated me extra special. I think they knew my secret. Once Mom left, dinner was my job. When I wasn't home, it was my brother's job. The only thing good about Mom not being at the table was I wasn't ridiculed about eating too much or, even worse, having to finish everything on my plate. When Mom was gone, we ate what we liked!

Once, I had a friend over, and I truly was not hungry, but it was dinner time. I just wanted to play with my friend. Mother insisted I eat dinner first. No wonder children can get so confused. Parents often send mixed messages to their children. Eat. Don't eat too much. Ignore it when you're hungry. Eat when you're not. So, like always, I ignored my body and tried to please my mother. My friend finished her plate. I sat staring down at mine. Mother insisted that if I didn't clean my plate, I could not go play with my friend. Well, I finished my plate of spaghetti. But when I got up from the table, pushed back my chair, and leaned over, it all came right back up onto the plate.

I was shocked. It looked like it had never been eaten. Fear gripped me. Embarrassment flooded my cheeks. Mother raised her voice and said, "You did that on purpose." My mind raced. *Can people really do that on purpose?* Then she said, "For two cents, I'd make you eat that again." I truly thought she would. I can't remember anything after that. *Did I go play with my friend? Did I clean up the dishes? What did my friend think? Or say?* I can't remember a lot of things about my childhood. I try. I can't—especially after Mother left.

When you are abandoned, the person or people who abandoned you take more than your bad memories; they take some of the good, too.

Today, I have a beautiful china cupboard full of beautiful dishes that my husband and I picked out together on our eighteenth wedding anniversary. We were too young and poor to register for china when we were married. But my husband knew the pattern I'd always wanted. So, one day, we went and picked it all out. I love to set a beautiful table. When Mother found out, her words still cut me. "Where is the meat plate?" We didn't get one. We thought we would get it at a later date. Our finances really couldn't afford all the extra pieces. Mother made a big deal out of it, and she purchased the meat platter for us. I slowly began to see my mother in a different light. But full illumination wouldn't come until much later.

I allow my grown children to fill their plates, and if they don't finish their plate, I'm good. We tend to want to give our children what we didn't have. I prefer a beautiful table set with china and glassware; my grown children prefer paper plates. I care more about them than I do my table settings. As I have journeyed through life, I have found that these things don't matter. They don't want to wash those dishes. Did I mention I have a dishwasher?

Times change. We must change with them.

I remember wanting my tennis shoes hung on the line so they would be white like Janie's mom did hers. I wanted my peanut butter and butter sandwich cut in fours and wrapped in wax paper like the girl on the school bus who would give me half her sandwich. I wanted a mother who took care of me like the other kid's mothers. Now, I see the good in learning all I learned during those years. I can find the silver lining in that cloud. I know how to do a lot of things and am very successful and grateful for what I learned. I don't wish that same type of education or schooling on anyone else, but it made me who I am today. I have no desire to be a victim. I am not looking for sympathy. My goal is understanding, healing, and growth.

I choose to be okay with how I grew up. I remind myself it is not all or nothing (Abandonment thinking). Take turns. Be present when others talk, even if everyone is talking all at once. Meals can still be challenging. I know it's okay to tell the grandchildren, "No, you can't have a Smucker's Uncrustable® (peanut butter and jelly round sandwich) after dinner. If you are still hungry, then eat more dinner." They can have a peanut butter and jelly round for a snack if they want one in an hour or two. They are growing boys; one is almost twelve years old, one is nine years old, and I have a four-year-old granddaughter who can out-eat them both! They are never full. But I am on to that peanut butter and jelly round trick-- though they did get me a few times.

I have also healed enough not to feel guilty if I do not finish my meal, even if it is at a costly restaurant. In fact, I usually ask for a box first off and only eat half my meal. In the past, I wouldn't let anyone have my leftovers, but I didn't eat them either. Now, I freely give them to whoever wants them. I am enough. I can buy more if I want. I do not have to hide or hoard food. I do not have to eat if I am not hungry for fear of an opportunity missed. I love this new freedom. My body is my body. I love it, and I do not want to harm it, even if it is unknowingly.

I feel I need to mention here that in my learning and searching for answers, I have found some answers for others that I was not seeking. For example, I have learned that many abandoned people have hoarding issues. In the *Journal of Obsessive-Compulsive and Related Disorders Volume 21*, an article states:

> *Based on previous research suggesting that childhood adversity is a risk factor for hoarding, it was first hypothesized that higher levels of childhood trauma would predict higher current levels of hoarding symptoms.*[4]

Hoarding, thankfully, has never been an issue with me. I have never overfilled my home or not been able to toss things. However, if it has personal feelings attached, I can still struggle, like with my blue jean jacket. I would say I hoard shoes. As a child, we got two new pairs when school started. We got tennis shoes (our gym shoes) and school shoes. Our old shoes became our play shoes. I would get in big trouble if I wore my school shoes to play in. But I wanted to be pretty. So sometimes, I would get yelled at for wearing my good shoes to play in. Well, today, I have more shoes than I can count. I have a pair of shoes for every outfit and at least one pair of running shoes of every brand made—except for the ugly ones. If you battle or know someone who has an issue with hoarding, it might be a good idea to give them a copy of this book. Wounded people wound people, and hoarders wound themselves and those who live with them. It is a dangerous issue, but there is hope.

I have suffered from gastrointestinal issues my entire life. In the past, I've been negligent to allow or even recognize normal bodily functions to happen naturally as our bodies are designed. I was the kid who waited until I got home from school. I realized this dates back to childhood experiences yet again. I would feel shame if someone even mentioned, "Who used the bathroom last?" I was embarrassed that I smelled up the bathroom. I was somehow dirty and smelly. I recalled while writing this book that once, on a mission trip, I shut down my body for a full 16 days. I was stressed and uncomfortable having to share a space with others. While traveling with the mission team, I felt a sense of shame in asking the driver to stop and inconvenience others. I would just ignore my body like so many times before.

Look, we are all human. We need to show kindness to others even if we don't understand them. This goes for you and me too. Give yourself permission to be a human. Don't ignore your appetites or your body. God gave them to us for a reason. If you have been abandoned or have ADHD, understand that what seems "normal" to others may not be normal for you and me. There is no shame in being different.

Give yourself permission to be a human.

It has been interesting how I can forget so many things and then try with all my might to forget other things. I have come to appreciate that I can remember things differently, and I can learn from them and grow. Though the scars of childhood abandonment may express themselves in the quietest, most private rituals—neglecting hunger, resisting rest, clinging to things when people felt unsafe—these patterns do not have to be life sentences. They are remnants of survival, once necessary, now ready to be understood and gently unraveled. Healing begins not with perfection but with permission: to listen to the body's signals without shame, to let go without fear, and to reclaim space with compassion. With awareness, support, and kindness, what once felt like chaos can become a source of wisdom, and what was once neglected can be nurtured into resilience. The past may have shaped the pattern, but it does not have to write the ending.

You are the author of your own story. You can rewrite the script starting today.

ENDNOTES

1. Bessel, van der Kolk, *The Body Keeps The Score* (New York: Penguin Books, 2014), 55.

2. Ibid., 55-56.

3. Ibid., 45.

4. Elizabeth, Kehoe, and Egan, Jonathan, "Interpersonal Attachment Insecurity and Emotional Attachment to Possessions Partly Mediate the Relationship Between Childhood Trauma and Hoarding Symptoms In A Non-Clinical Sample, *Journal of Obsessive-Compulsive and Related Disorders,* Volume 21, 2019, 37-45.

C H A P T E R   S I X

How Abandonment Affects Health

"The past can tick away inside us for decades like a silent time bomb until it sets off a cellular message that lets us know the body does not forget the past."

DONNA JACKSON NAKAZAWA,
CHILDHOOD DISRUPTED

Living on high alert is exhausting. Living to please others and performing takes a lot out of you. Expressing agreement with others when you don't actually agree for fear of conflict or being abandoned yet again is repeated trauma.

These things take energy. Keeping silent when you want to scream or disagree puts your stomach in knots. The tension you hold inside you at night when you sleep can cause ringing in your ears, and clenching your teeth so tight that they ache to the point that when you wake up, you are too tired to function. Yes, all too familiar. Abandonment does affect our health.

SLEEP ISSUES

Repeated nightmares of falling and waking up at the slightest sound, thinking someone is in your room, cause your body not to recover well. You may fight inflammation in your joints, which causes pain and weight gain from the extra cortisol in your system. The hypervigilance is always burning extra fuel, not to mention the damage it does to your vital organs, and so, some days, you are just burnt out. I get it. Abandonment can cause PTSD and can even become C-PTSD (Complex Post-Traumatic Stress Disorder), which was my case, along with anxiety and ADHD, which can bring on bouts of depression.

In *Assessing Psychological Trauma and PTSD*, John Wilson and Terence Keane observe:

> *The PTSD D1 hyperarousal criterion (difficulty falling or staying asleep) reflects sleep disturbances and includes disruptions of the early, middle, or terminal phase of the cycle. Accompanying the difficulties with sleeping are night sweats, problems returning to sleep upon early awakening, nightmares, night terrors, somnambulism, agitation, and restless activity while sleeping,*

which may be attended by vocalizations (e.g., gasps, screams, crying, talking, making references to the trauma experience, etc.).[1]

BREATHING ISSUES

If trouble sleeping was not enough—so was breathing. I fought asthma all my life. I never knew I even had asthma until I had to have a check-up for a job. Remember I learned early to ignore my body. The doctor asked me if I always wheezed. I told him I never had a problem. I was diagnosed with asthma and given an inhaler. I remember while in Bible College, a well-known leading evangelist of the times was identifying spirits of infirmity and had said, "Asthma is from a Spirit of Abandonment." That hit me hard. I decided if it were a spirit, I would fight it in prayer and get delivered. I did, but it always seemed to come back. The only times I deal with it now are when I eat a dairy product, go from cold to hot temperatures, or when the air is too dry or too cold. I've got it under control … until … I get triggered. If people around me that I love start getting into a heated discussion, my body starts to feel tense. I start to notice that I clear my throat a lot and cough. It's still a trigger. From *The Body Keeps the Score*:

> *Traumatized people chronically feel unsafe inside their bodies. The past is alive in the form of gnawing interior discomfort. Their bodies are constantly bombarded by visceral warning signs, and, in an attempt to control these processes,*

they often become experts at ignoring their gut feelings and numbing awareness of what is played out inside. They learn to hide from their selves.[2]

It's only been since my journey from abandonment to acceptance that I could even make this correlation—*abandonment affects your health.* I was living it, but I just didn't realize the connection. I began putting those puzzle pieces together, finally aware that I'm not always dealing with the "now;" sometimes I am dealing with what "was." What *was* in my past keeps showing up in my here and now.

> I had no idea it was abnormal to live like I was living.

What *was* in my past, I am still trying to process. I was unaware that I was **not** okay. I thought I was okay. I thought the way I was living was normal. It was my normal. I had no idea it was abnormal to live like I was living. I was able to fool everyone, including myself, for a long time. But, one day, the **not** okay could not be ignored any longer. It, whatever that "it" was, was demanding to be reckoned with. It had affected my health for years. I was tired of not feeling well and doctors being unable to diagnose me with something, anything!

All the tests always came back normal. Everything was always chalked off as a female issue, a hormone issue, or "We don't see anything wrong" until I began to think I was crazy. I was not crazy. I was abandoned—many times. When

I was given a diagnosis of ADHD and Childhood Trauma, this probably sounds bizarre, but I was relieved! Relieved because I *finally* had an answer to *why* I had the feelings and thoughts that I had. There was a reason *why* I was so filled with anxiety my entire life and why I acted the way I did. All the "whys" were finally getting answered.

GUT ISSUES

I have lived a life battling severe constipation, chronic abdominal pain with no specific diagnosis associated with the pain, acid reflux, frequent heartburn, and a recent diagnosis of diverticulitis. In an article posted by the NIH about trauma and the gut, I read:

> *Functional gastrointestinal disorders form an important healthcare burden in Western societies. In one of their most common manifestations, the irritable bowel syndrome (IBS), there is evidence for altered visceral sensory and motor responses to stimuli. Psychiatric disturbances may determine the degree to which symptoms are experienced as stressful or debilitating. Traumatic experiences could have a role in the aetiology or perception of IBS, and there are indications that functional gastrointestinal disorders are a common occurrence in patients with post-traumatic stress disorder (PTSD).*

Motility, sensitivity, and psychology

Functional gastrointestinal disorders represent a combination of chronic or recurrent gastrointestinal symptoms that cannot be explained by structural or biochemical abnormalities. These comprise esophageal disorders, including functional ('non-cardiac') chest pain, gastro-duodenal disorders, including functional dyspepsia, bowel disorders, including IBS, and functional biliary and anorectal disorders. Current diagnostic criteria for the IBS are restricted to a combination of abdominal pain (associated with defecation or changed bowel habit), disordered defecation, and abdominal distention.[3]

Once, I remember I was miserable because I could not empty my bowels. I was on heightened alert. I was the only Caucasian woman in a large church of thousands in Eldoret, Kenya. Previously, when my youngest daughter was two years old, I was mugged at 2:30 p.m. in a parking garage in Pittsburgh, PA, by an African American man. After that, I was afraid of African American men. However, after I was in Kenya for a while teaching at the Bible College, I fell in love with the students. I had lost the all-or-nothing thinking and realized that not all dark-skinned men wanted to mug a young Caucasian woman any more than any other ethnicity. I had experienced a supernatural healing from God. The man who mugged me served his time in prison. My proverbial table of abandonment stood on the legs of fear, rejection, and low self-esteem. With that leg of fear removed, my table of abandonment was no longer able to stand between me and living my best life.

Constipation can still be an issue for me because, with ADHD, I often forget to eat and drink when I get hyper-focused; I know that. So, I set reminders for myself. I tell a friend to call me and check in with me. I have learned to work with my body and help myself with the way my brain and body communicate. John Bradshaw shares:

> As the child from the dysfunctioning family grows up, these survival behaviors continue even though they are now disconnected from the original source of distress. These survival behaviors feel normal since they are the patterns the family member used every day of his early life in order to survive. As an adult, they are not only unnecessary; they are actually unhealthy. While once they were protective, now they are destructive.[4]

JOINTS AND MUSCLES

The other thing abandonment and childhood emotional neglect can cause is for you to carry stress in certain parts of your body. For me, it is in my shoulders and back. Whenever

I would get overly stressed, rushed, or pressured, I tended to bring my shoulders up to my ears. Literally, the space between my shoulders and earlobes disappeared. I would have so much lactic acid build up in my shoulders that I vomited after a massage. The masseuse warned me to drink lots of water to flush the lactic acid out of my system that she had broken down and massaged out of the lumps in my neck and shoulders. I guess I didn't drink enough water. *Does anyone ever drink "enough" water?* Everything I learned, I seemingly had to learn the hard way. What I mean by this is that *everything* came with consequences, and they were usually negative. I had no one to tell me to relax except my husband. He told me constantly. *But how do you do that?* I wondered. No one noticed until later in life that my shoulders were in my ears. Today, I consciously stop and take deep breaths and relax my shoulders and joints. I have had cervical spine surgery and am learning to pay attention to how I am feeling, but this has all come at a very high cost, emotionally, physically, and financially.

Leslie Sokol and Marci Fox explain it like this:

> *At any given moment of the day, each of us is exposed to a multitude of external and internal experiences. External stimuli are those things going on around us. Internal stimuli are the sensations that we experience inside our bodies or minds. Both sets of experiences can set off doubt. How we process these experiences is influenced*

by our underlying self-doubt. Do we see them in a neutral way or as a sign of danger and distress?[5]

In the past, I experienced life through an unconscious negative filter. Today, I live with an intentionally renewed mind. I have come to learn in my research and studies that stimuli, external or internal, are just that, stimuli. The day I was mugged was a sunny, hot day. The external and internal stimuli affected me to the point I drove the 90 minutes home without turning the air conditioning on in 90° weather. The control switch in my brain and body malfunctioned. Thankfully, I arrived home safely.

Because I ignored my bodily functions, the aches, the pains, and the normal functions of all humans, I have almost died several times. Did you know those with neglect, trauma, and ADHD die earlier than those who have not been diagnosed? In a 2025 article from *The British Journal of Psychiatry*, I learned scientists had discovered in their research that:

The apparent reduction in life expectancy for adults with diagnosed ADHD relative to the general population was 6.78 years for males and 8.64 years for females. The conclusion is that adults with diagnosed ADHD are living shorter lives than they should. We believe that this is likely caused by modifiable risk factors and unmet support and treatment needs in terms of both ADHD and co-occurring mental and physical health conditions.

This study included data from adults with diagnosed ADHD; the results may not generalize to the entire population of adults with ADHD, the vast majority of whom are undiagnosed. Diagnoses of common physical and mental health conditions were more common in adults with diagnosed ADHD than the comparison group. Their research conclusion, adults with diagnosed ADHD are living shorter lives than they should.[6]

MENTAL AND EMOTIONAL HEALTH

Abandonment has also affected my emotional health. I have experienced great difficulty connecting with others, even those I love the most. My emotional pendulum swings wide. I rarely share anything personal, or because of my history and ADHD, I share more than some would care to know or I would care to tell. Then I experience guilt and shame to the point I have conversations with myself. It was fine for others to share with me, but I wouldn't trust anyone enough to let them truly know me for fear of rejection. They may have thought they knew me, and many thought they did, but they only knew the performer or the person I portrayed—my imposter. I could not let anyone get close, which affected my relationships, but that's the next chapter.

I noticed when people started talking about emotions, I would make jokes or change the subject. I was an expert at deflecting and was often accused of changing the subject or avoiding emotional topics. I finally realized I was ashamed because I thought there was something truly wrong with me that no one could fix. I was broken beyond repair. The shame came from the wound of abandonment. John Bradshaw explains it like this:

> Shame is at the heart of our wound and differs greatly from the feeling of guilt. Guilt says I've done something wrong; shame says there is something wrong with me. Guilt says, I've made a mistake; shame says I am a mistake. Guilt says what I did was not good; shame says I am no good.[7]

I could never take compliments well. I usually laughed or made a joke about how inexpensive something was, or I told people that it was a gift. I have learned the hard way to simply say, "Thank you." A quote attributed to Tania Luna helps me understand this phenomenon:

> This intense emotional experience can feel uncomfortable and destabilizing. And, as a result, some of us may want to shut it down so we can feel stable and get comfortable again. Deflecting other's praise by quickly blurting out an awkward response could be an unconscious way of trying

to regain control in what feels like an emotionally vulnerable situation.[8]

For me, this was, and oftentimes is still the case when I am not rested or taking care of myself. However, being aware of an issue and admitting there is an issue is half the battle.

In Nedra Glover Tawwab's book *Drama Free,* the author introduces the book by stating the following:

> *Among the most significant contributions to your mental health, relationships can cause you pain, or they can heal you. Positively or negatively, relationships have an impact on your mental and emotional well-being. Psychologists have long supported the finding that healthy relationships can prolong your life, while unhealthy ones can influence health issues like cancer, heart disease, depression, anxiety, and addiction. So, we must take the health of our relationships seriously and strengthen connections where possible.*[9]

I have read so much about abandonment, and honestly, I can relate. As you are reading, I am sure you can, too. I have read we have more accidents. Yep, who falls inside a dishwasher, trips over a rug, and breaks their nose? Who actually thinks they can just close one eye and keep driving and stay awake? I know, right? Who has ever lost their phone and had a panic attack because they can't find it and proceeded to pull over off of a major highway and open the door to look for their phone while talking on it?

People who are abandoned have a shorter lifespan. I can understand why!

> *"Trauma creates change you don't choose. Healing is about creating change you do choose."*
> MICHELLE ROSENTHALL

I often avoided difficult conversations or confronting others for fear of being abandoned. Only recently have I mastered or at least tried to begin difficult conversations using "I" statements over "you" statements. An invaluable resource for my growth in the area of cognitive functioning can be found at the Beck Institute of Cognitive Behavior Therapy, where a variety of resources can be found.[10] I encourage you, if you are in the habit of using "you" statements in conversations and even self-talk, to check out the website and start changing your life with the decision to change one word in your vocabulary at a time. We can only implement the knowledge we know into our lives. The counseling techniques of Dr. Aaron Beck's Cognitive Behavior Therapy (CBT) and his other resources have been a tremendous help in my relationships with those closest to me. I am now able to be heard without others becoming defensive. With others becoming less defensive, I am less on guard and able to stay present in the conversation.

Intimacy has been quite difficult. It takes me a long time to trust, open up, and be vulnerable. I often laugh and say that's why my marriage has worked—because my husband of over 48 years is still trying to get to know me and figure me out!

Probably the most troublesome thing is how I totally dissociate when a situation is uncomfortable, frightening, threatening, or triggers me. I honestly will forget I went somewhere. I will remember one detail but can't remember who was there, what I said, or the details. This used to frighten me because I thought I had dementia or Alzheimer's disease. I once woke up after a traumatic event and called a friend in sheer panic because I could not remember details from the night before except for one significant conversation. My friend assured me that I lived the moment and that I was present. My brain checked out, and I performed, and that's why I couldn't remember the less significant moments of the evening or recall all the details.

When I get significantly stressed or overloaded, I tend to brain-dump to survive. I just go somewhere without ever moving from my physical location, and all the while, no one will know I've checked out. Those closest to me don't usually have a clue--that's what makes it so scary. During this entire healing process, I have learned how to stay present. I name five things I see. I will identify five things I feel, and I take slow, deep breaths. I will repeat what someone said so I can hear it again and get clarity. I will stand up and stretch. All of these work for me ... most of the time.

Before my journey to healing from abandonment, I would never share a conflicting opinion. I would just dismiss myself, which made me appear haughty, too good, insensitive, or uncaring. Truth be known, I was just trying to survive. I couldn't find my voice. The voice I could find wasn't kind or caring to me. So, I would quickly agree with those who were too boisterous or frightening to me. I went along to get along. Being untrue to myself only made me like myself less and endorsed the feeling of worthlessness.

> Being untrue to myself only made me like myself less and endorsed the feeling of worthlessness.

Abandonment and ADHD have taken their toll on me in my mind. I can become so fixated on something that I become totally unaware of my surroundings. I frequently obsess and loop when I can't find something important to me or figure something out. I find myself caught up in this trauma loop I can't get out of. I get anxious because I can't trust the information others give me or that I give myself. Hence, the blue jean jacket in chapter one. All I could think of was my jacket. I literally remember nothing about that fourteen-hour trip except my jacket.

I overreact to traumatic events. I am frightened easily. If I receive a phone call unexpectedly, I would jump to the worst-case scenario. If I called someone and they didn't answer they were either mad at me or dead. I am getting better. I just get on the hamster wheel and run in no particular or predetermined direction when frightened. I would look for something in the same places repeatedly until I exhausted myself. I frequently scream when startled or surprised in an overly dramatic way. I literally scare others, which is not appreciated. I know better, but I still have trouble controlling this reaction. It takes practice and patience. I now catch myself, and that alone is a huge deal for me. I am learning to celebrate the small wins. I give myself love and care when I go into panic mode and soothe myself. No matter where you are in your **#abandonedtoo** journey, there is hope. There are tools. There is help.

You may be asking, how do I do that? As an adult of CEN (childhood emotional neglect) and abandonment with adult-diagnosed ADHD, I learned some techniques and am in the process of learning more. Remember, I've still got that "I've got to be the best thing going on." Here's my autopilot "Go To." I rub my pointer finger and thumb together on both hands, as I shared in an earlier chapter, something I noticed my father doing. I also shake my left leg to fall asleep. During waking hours, I jiggle my foot or bounce my knee, now realizing that these are all self-soothing techniques.

While continuing to do my own research to heal myself, I found William Glasser's book on Reality Therapy. As a pastor, I often format my sermons in three points. This is one of the reasons this therapy grabbed my attention. Glasser wrote the book on Reality Therapy and the three R's—Reality, Responsibility, and Right. Glasser writes that:

To lead patients toward reality, toward grappling successfully with the tangible and intangible aspects of the real world, and might accurately be called a therapy toward reality, or simply Reality Therapy.[11]

Glasser's view of the therapy process was not stating what is RIGHT or WRONG, but rather that the individual, through the process of Reality Therapy, would make choices to change behaviors through "self-evaluation" and become Responsible. Glasser dismisses concerns about things beyond what we can't control, such as other people's behavior, negative experiences or past events, and the notion of right versus wrong, but rather for people to do what they decide to do in view of their beliefs, culture, society, and values. He defines the third R (Right) as Religion and Spirituality. Glasser places faith and spirituality as behaviors chosen to satisfy needs. On the other hand, he allows for faith as a need but not as one of *his* formulations. Reality Therapy helps the person function in a different way, notwithstanding the misfortunes in the patient's past.[12]

COPING MECHANISMS

I remember once, on a trip to Kenya, I was feeling overwhelmed and stressed. I was in the back seat and started shaking my leg. A pastor friend was with me and spoke up and said, "Do you feel that?"

"Feel what?" I asked.

"Are we having an earthquake?"

I paused a minute to get my bearings and felt the car. "No, I don't think so," I responded. I went back to shaking my leg.

She said, "There, I feel it again."

I realized I was shaking the entire car. So, making light of a "could-be bad moment," I stopped shaking my leg and asked her, "Do you still feel it?"

She answered, "No."

So, I did it again and looked at her and laughed and said, "It's me over here enjoying my own private earthquake."

Another time, I was on a mission trip with a ministry friend. We settled in to get some sleep after a long, stressful day. I began shaking my leg to soothe myself to sleep. My also high-intensity type-A personality friend said to me, "I'm so glad you shake your leg to go to sleep—now I won't have to." We shared a good laugh and joked about it for years.

Abandoned and emotionally neglected children don't grow up naturally to be confident and well-equipped adults. They can stay in the Blame Cycle and refuse to take responsibility for learning what they don't know rather than learn and train themselves to use grounding techniques and tools to calm themselves down. We can either be totally unaware of our issue or be clueless that it even is an issue. I have had an IQ test, and my IQ was above average, so I am not at all shy about exposing my issues. I am just so grateful I can fully love and appreciate myself and thank the good Lord that I am fearfully and wonderfully made. I have survived and even thrived in some areas of my life.

> *"Healing doesn't mean the damage never existed. It means the damage no longer controls our lives."*
>
> AKSHAY DUBEY

HEALING IS UP TO US

To become healthier, it's going to cost you. It will cost you time, money, and hard work. It will cost you emotionally to take risks that are out of your comfort zone and maybe even get you hundreds of "Nos" before a "Yes." Just ask *Chicken Soup for the Soul* author Jack Canfield, also a native West Virginian. I can't quote him exactly, but in my memory, I hear him say, "We have to put on our 'I can take correction' or 'I can take rejection' suit. Zip it up, and get up out of bed, and face the day with a smile."

Sometimes, not knowing all the rules and information works in one's favor. I sold a car to a guy who didn't have a driver's license. I sold another car to a guy who wanted a red car, but I only had a blue car on the lot. I told him his eyes matched the car, and he looked great sitting in it. I wasn't a trained salesman. I knew nothing about selling cars. I was just being me and minding my husband's car lot while he was away on a mission trip. I was myself. But, for most of my life, *not knowing* a vital piece of information or just being myself has caused me much pain, both emotionally and physically.

I thought I was just different. I am. **Being different is okay.** My life experiences have made me who I am. Don't allow ignorance or comparison to keep you from living your best life. Maybe what you are called to do has never been done before. Be you. I remember hearing that Walt Disney was told by his art teacher that flowers don't have faces. His answer was, "Mine do." Ever been to Disney? Aren't you glad Walt was okay with being different? He had a pretty traumatic upbringing, too!

As we continue together through this journey of abandonment to acceptance, I invite you to consider the words of Sokol and Fox in *Think Confident, Be Confident:*

> *For a new confidence belief to take hold, it is important that you not trip yourself up by using isolated events to deconstruct it. Most of us do not realize that we tend to focus on a specific or a series of specific moments in time to define who we are as a person. Focusing on those moments leads to broad, inaccurate conclusions of doubt. Instead, focusing on the summation of many moments leads to a more valid and a more confident view. The goal is to help you look at yourself through the*

lens of confidence rather than through the lens of those magnified moments of doubt. [13]

Listen, the things you have gone through were not fair, and they have deeply impacted you. Let me encourage you that healing is possible. God desires you to be whole—to live in peace. You don't need to pretend what happened wasn't real. You don't need to downplay it or explain it. Acknowledging it is not entitled. You are not using it as a crutch or as an excuse for unacceptable behavior. But accepting and sharing your story is about reclaiming what is yours—what has always been yours: your worth, your voice, and your future.

Healing is not a straight line, but every step you take in the right direction tells your past that it does not get to dictate your future. You are at the helm of your destiny, and you have the power to steer the ship of purpose into your next port of call.

Your physical, mental, emotional, relational, and spiritual health are yours to steward. The journey from this day forward is in your hands. Take it at your own pace, but always remember that healing is an option you can choose.

I hope you will.

ENDNOTES

1. John and Kean, Wilson. Terence. *Assessing Psychological Trauma and PTSD*. (New York: 2004). 27

2. Bessel, van der Kolk, The Body Keeps The Score (New York: Penguin Books, 2014),

3. Stam, R., Akkermans, L.M., Wiegant, V.M., "Trauma and the gut: interactions between stressful experience and intestinal function." Review, courtesy of BMJ Publishing Group from PMC PubMed Central® from the NIH National Library of Medicine. Posted onhttps://pmc.ncbi.nlm.nih.gov/articles/PMC1027192/ retrieved on May 08, 2025.

4. Bradshaw, John. *Bradshaw On: The Family*. (Deerfield Beach: Health Communications, Inc., 1996), 184.

5. Leslie, Sokol, Ph.D., Marci G., Fox, Ph.D. *Think Confident, Be Confident*. (New York: Penguin Group). 2009, 12

6. *The British Journal of Psychiatry* "Life Expectancy and Years of Life Lost for Adults with Diagnosed ADHD in the UK: Matched Cohort Study." (2025). p. 1 of 8. doi: 10.1192/bjp.2024.199.

7. Bradshaw, John. *Bradshaw On: The Family* (Deerfield Beach: Health Communications, Inc., 1996), 2-3.

8. This quote is attributed to Tania Luna, co-host of the podcast *Talk Psych to Me*.

9. Nedra Glover, Tawwab. *Drama Free: A Guide to Managing Unhealthy Family Relationships*. TarcherPerigee, an Imprint of Penguin Random House LLC, 2023.

10. Visit: https://beckinstitute.org/ for incredible resources.

11. William, Glasser. *Reality Therapy. (New York: HarperCollins)*, 2010. 6.

12. Ibid. 20, 61.

13. Leslie, Sokol, Ph.D., Marci G., Fox, Ph.D. *Think Confident, Be Confident*. (New York: Penguin Group). 2009. 154.

CHAPTER SEVEN

How Abandonment Affects Wealth

"If you expect nothing from somebody,
you are never disappointed."

SYLVIA PLATH, *THE BELL JAR*

The abandonment I experienced during my childhood was keeping me from making money. I was sabotaging myself with low self-esteem, fear, feelings of worthlessness, and that overwhelming sense of never being good enough. Worse yet, I expected nothing. I told myself nothing would work out. Keep your expectations low. Don't get excited; that way, you won't get disappointed.

So, I was living with a poverty mindset—my beliefs and behaviors perpetuated financial struggle and sabotaged any financial success. In short, I was making less money than I was capable of making. In the Bible, tax collectors approached Peter to collect a temple tax. Jesus told Peter to go fishing and that when he opened the mouth of the first fish he hooked, he would find a coin in the fish's mouth. Then, Peter could use the money to pay the taxes.[1] Now, stay with me for a moment. You would agree that Jesus made us to be fishers of men. If that is true, and if we apply the story of the coin in the fish's mouth, then the money we need can be found in the mouths of others (the fish) we catch. Allow me to explain.

While writing this book, I became acquainted with someone who works at Vacation Resort. Let's call her Karen. I was sharing with her about what I was doing all week. "Writing my fourth book," I said. She then asked about the topic and my title, and as I began to explain, I could tell she was listening intently. I had caught a fish. At the end of our conversation, she asked, "When does your book come out?"

I said, "Prayerfully by August."

"How can I get a copy?" she asked. I gave her my website. I had just found a coin in the mouth of a fish. I don't really know Karen, but do we ever really know a fish? Not always, because sometimes we are only given a brief, one-time first impression to share what may be the chance of a lifetime.

SEIZE THE OPPORTUNITIES

"Opportunities are like sunrises.
If you wait too long, you miss them."
WILLIAM ARTHUR WARD

I cannot count the sunrises I have missed because of procrastination, toxic immobility, the fear of rejection, an overwhelming sense of performance anxiety, and the list goes on. I had dreams. I had these grandiose visions for my life, but I just couldn't seem to move on them. That was my life. I failed in my mind and heart and soul before ever getting started. Then, if someone believed in me, if they could hold my hand and tell me how to get from point A to point B and not overwhelm me with all the details, I found I could do it. My reaction to stress and danger would subside. It was going to be okay. The more I accepted and repeated the process of allowing others to help me and to allow myself to count on them, to experience the reality that some people stay till the end, some people don't leave, some people really want you around, some people believe in you—I began to heal. My scars began to fade. I was on my way from abandonment to acceptance.

Before my journey through the process of healing from abandonment, I would automatically assume that whoever I met didn't like me. Looking back, it seems crazy. How can a person not like you when they don't even know you?

If a spouse has abandoned you, if your parents have distanced themselves because of your differing beliefs or lifestyle, or if an employer penalized you or pushed you away because of a cutback or a differing stance on a subject, such was the case during COVID, you may very well have taken it personally. Because the truth of the matter is—it is personal. Very personal. It hurts. It leaves us scared. Did you ever catch yourself staring at someone's scars? I have. I was uncomfortable when they caught my glance, but I am sure they were even more uncomfortable because I focused on what was a reminder of something painful.

LIMITING BELIEFS PUT LIMITS ON YOUR INCOME

Well, in the area of finances, my scars were showing. Even if they were carefully tucked away under my polished exterior, it was as though I felt everyone had x-ray vision. I felt like they were thinking I was an imposter because—I was. After all, I had to be an imposter because, in and of myself, no one would ever be interested in anything I had to offer. Right? Abandonment wounds go deep. The closer those that abandoned us were, the uglier the scar. So, even before a deal or an opportunity was offered to me, I expected nothing. I would offer them a back out—a "get out of relationship with me for free" card. It's okay if you can't keep your word. It's okay if you never call. I understand. I am ugly. I am scarred. I am less important than other things in your life.

This thought pattern was completely unconscious. I had no idea that I was doing this until I decided to take a class to help others write a book and increase their income. As a pastor, I have a great desire to help others. I have earned the nickname "the Resource Queen." I have never charged anyone for anything, but I have paid greatly for what I have learned. I would spend countless hours researching a subject and then not get paid for the information I shared. I wouldn't charge a fee; after all, I am not valuable. Of course, this was not the truth, but the voice of abandonment had my ear. If I did get paid a small honorarium or fee, I would say, "Well, at least I got paid something." I never complained, but inside, I kept lowering my worth.

I discovered I was not alone:

> *A recent study published in the* American Journal of Family Economic Issues *showed that people who had experienced one or more types of adverse childhood experiences (ACEs) were more likely to demonstrate decreases in financial well-being …*

> *Early childhood trauma impairs later developing executive functioning. Executive functioning creates reflection, planning, and organizing. Basically, it's what makes you a fully functional adult capable of being emotionally mature, maintaining intimate relationships, and flourishing at work.*

An estimated two-thirds of children who have been neglected or abused don't grow up to be functional adults because they can't think through things like their career plans or organize their finances. The lack of executive functioning means that most abused and neglected children never really reach their full adult functioning capabilities.

One study showed that individuals with a history of childhood maltreatment had more trouble making complex financial decisions than those without such histories.[2]

In another article by Cynthia and John Harter, I found myself self-identifying with the terminology of adverse childhood experiences and with the conclusion found in their research that having experienced more ACEs is correlated with having more financial stress in adulthood as measured by food security and housing security. These results suggest that it is not only physical and mental health that is negatively impacted by ACEs, but it is also financial well-being. "[3]

I decided there was probably something I didn't know, and if I didn't know it, well, I couldn't teach others. I believed that I was everyone's glass ceiling. I was the reason my congregation wasn't making more money. I was the reason they weren't reaching their potential. The self-talk of abandonment, being the firstborn, having an over-developed sense of responsibility for others, being trained during my formative years to believe that everything was always my fault if something went wrong. I was responsible for my little brothers. I felt responsible for making Dad happy. In her book *Thou Shalt Not Be Aware*, Alice Miller said, "An unacknowledged trauma is like a wound that never heals over and may start to bleed again at any time." Well, all these feelings were bleeding into all my financial opportunities. For them to grow, I would have to grow. I finally realized I was only responsible for myself. Everything is not my fault. The weight of the world is not on my shoulders.

I am still in the process of learning to release the controlling spirit that had such a grip on me. I controlled because I was afraid—afraid of little things that kept my anxiety fueled. When I felt that anxiety rise up, instead of pushing it back down, I would breathe and talk to myself. Then, I started noticing little things. I would tell people when to make a left or to go straight when they were driving because I took over the responsibility of getting us to the right location. I wasn't even driving! Who did I think I was? How disrespectful? If someone was sad, I felt as though I had to somehow make them feel better. Not my job. I overstepped my boundaries constantly. This caused me to be rejected again and again. I was caught in a vicious cycle. My wanting to help was heartfelt. I seriously was trying my best. I just didn't know what I didn't know. However, this was the first time being over-responsible paid off. My own dysfunction drove me to enroll in this class. I seized the opportunity, and it changed my life. I am still changing. I am not the savior of the world. I am learning to breathe. Let go. Trust.

However, once again, no one encouraged me—just like I expected. Alone again. No one said, "That's a great idea," or "I'll help you." Nope. No one. But this time, I decided to finally do something for me. Yes, I enrolled in that class. Hands soaking wet and my heart beating out of my chest, I filled out the forms and hit send. It was a big sum of money for me. My husband said that he would support me emotionally but couldn't help financially. I found those old feelings of being abandoned yet again, and I felt like I was completely on my own. Panic came soaring in. The lack of finances was hitting me in the face. I thought a lot about my situation, and of course, I prayed. But in all honesty, I also called to whine to my pastor, and she said, "Well, if you want to do it, then you are going to have to exercise your faith muscle and believe God for it."

I thought to myself, *Even my pastor won't help me! I am left alone—abandoned yet again.* I was looping. But that's what I did! I believed God wanted me to further my education, and that's exactly where God met me. The money came in. I found out I was no longer the pretender or performer; the class helped me to be me. I found my voice. I discovered my authentic self. I had difficult life experiences, but that was part of what made me—me. I quit trying to impress people with all I knew so they wouldn't abandon me. I stopped spoon-feeding them the twenty-plus hours I had researched for a message that only lasted 45 minutes. Instead, I looked to connect. I looked to leave them with the hope I had long ago given up on getting myself. I took off the mask. I stopped performing like that otter at the zoo. I didn't seek the applause or accolades of men. I simply shared my story—real and raw.

To my surprise, I began making four times the money I had made in previous years! I connected. They liked me. They liked me for me. We made genuine eye contact and connection. My value increased in my mind and heart first—and *then* in my income. I realized that wealth does not come from just preparation, research, knowledge, and timing; it comes with believing your own worth and value. It comes with authenticity. No one wants a

> **Wealth does not come from just preparation, research, knowledge, and timing ...**

fake dollar bill, a fake diamond ring, a knock off pair of that famous brand shoe. People are willing to pay for real. People want what it took you a lifetime to learn. People are willing to invest themselves in learning by "OPE" (other people's experiences) so they don't have to make the same mistakes.

Just because I had been abandoned, I was no less valuable. I quit looking for my worth in what happened to me and started getting my worth from what God said about me. I started seeing myself through the lenses of being valuable, beautiful, kind, intelligent, successful, capable, and fearless. This was not easy. I began to recite a list of affirmation statements that I said every day. I began to take people at their word instead of listening to the scenario in my head from past experiences that screamed you can't relax. Something bad is going to happen. Allow me to help you understand why I felt this way. My parents never fought. I never remember them screaming at one another. There was never obvious strife in my home growing up. My parents seemed to be in love. We were happy. Then, that one day. That one letter. Everything changed. I changed. I started living on high alert because I just knew something bad was going to happen. I just never knew when.

In her book *Trauma and Survival, Post-Traumatic and Dissociative Disorders in Women*, Elizabeth A. Waites writes:

> *Learning to live with such dilemmas lays the foundations for coping that can have a decisive impact on subsequent trauma reactions. When negative expectations have come to be an inevitable part of existence, specific traumatic events merely confirm long-standing beliefs about personal powerlessness. But hopeless giving-up is only one trauma response in the human repertory. Unlike defeated rats and mice, human beings tend to assimilate their defeats to complex ideas about themselves, their abilities, and their self-worth.*[4]

Discovering my worth and finding my voice was a slow and painful process. One event unraveled for me a knotted tapestry of how I saw myself and my subsequent actions. The administrative assistant to the coach in the class I took opened my eyes to a blind spot I'd had for years. Let's call her Sue. Sue called me one day and told me I really hurt her feelings and that she was ready to, in her own words, "Write me off." Then she said, "But I knew your story, so I decided to talk to you directly." She shared how I had hurt her feelings and how I had offended her. She continued, even though my heart was screaming, "Stop, I can't take any more truth—you are killing me! That was *never* my intention." But I remained silent as she shared her feelings, another thing new to me. People do that, you know? They share with others how they feel. Hmmm, I thought they just left—they just abandoned you—they just walked away.

My innate behavioral and personality traits have wired me in such a way that I can just cut people off and pretend they are dead. It came easy to me. I saw it done. It was done to me. But Sue was different. She said she genuinely liked me. No one had ever taken the time to dialog with me and *show me* what I couldn't see. I even told her—once the truth sank in, "I give people a 'get out of relationship with me for free card' every time I meet them, feel a connection, or feel that we could somehow help each other. I am really sorry."

See, I never reached into the mouth of the fish and caught the coin; I was more a "catch and release" type of fisherman. My thoughts sounded like this: *After all, the big ones always get away (my mom, my dad). Why bother fishing anyway? Just forget about your dreams. Forget about any connections. When you walk away, they will forget you ever lived, let alone your name. There won't be a second time you meet. Let them go quickly before you get hurt—before you are abandoned.*

I apologized to Sue on the phone that day. I didn't make an excuse; I simply shared where I was coming from, and she understood. She is one of the many reasons I wrote this book. It's for all the Sues in my life and for all the people I hurt, dismissed, excused, and offended for fear of being abandoned. For all the coins in the fishes' mouths I failed to catch, Lord put me on the catch-up plan. Restore me in the area of finances, Lord.

MY SEAT AT THE TABLE

Another way that abandonment affects our wealth is in all the times we fail to seize an opportunity as I mentioned earlier. I want to go a bit deeper. I'll call it "sitting at the big table." See, when I was young, there were five of us. My aunt had nine children, and most all Daddy's family members had at least four children, so at family gatherings, all the adults sat at the "Big Table," and the kids, including me, sat at the "Kid's Table." As I grew and more ministry opportunities came, I was usually asked to come up front, sit on the front row, or even take a seat at the "Big Table." I was honored, but I usually didn't travel alone, which meant I would have to leave my friends in the back—at "The Kid's Table" while I moved up front. For the most part, I declined. I didn't know my possible new connections could have benefitted us all. My low self-esteem, worth, and abandonment issues kept me at the "Kid's Table."

God only knows how many opportunities I missed because I felt I had nothing to bring to the table, let alone have my very own seat. The anxiety from the abandonment and the undiagnosed ADHD made me socially awkward. Even if no one noticed because of my Imposter Syndrome, I knew it; I could feel it. So, my hands would get soaked with sweat and ice cold. Then my feet would start freezing. If I felt the urge to speak, it would often be an interruption rather than a participation, for fear I would forget my thought. Or worse yet, due to me being uncomfortable in my own skin, I would change the subject. Mind you I was not aware of the fact I was doing this.

I had to be repeatedly corrected or given the look of "I will kill you later" to realize I'd done something unacceptable. With ADHD and the abandonment trauma, I wasn't learning and retaining what I had done wrong because I wasn't really present. I had learned in my early life of trauma to dissociate. I would be there, but I wasn't fully present. I wouldn't even remember the situation or event. I went into this protection mode and somehow managed to look like I was highly functioning, but in reality, I was not able to spin all the plates. They were shattering on the floor. So, the pattern was repeated—to my own detriment.

I wasn't learning and retaining what I had done wrong because I wasn't really present.

Dissociation is when you are not all there.

It is most often a disconnection from your body, your feelings, or your environment. We all have small experiences of dissociation, like when we zone out and do something on auto pilot, withdrawing our conscious attention and presence. For those with trauma in their backgrounds, this dissociation is both more frequent and more disconcerting.

Dissociation often comes on suddenly. It is a circuit breaker for a nervous system that has been overwhelmed. Dissociation is an emergency response that is only partially successful in managing the feelings of being overwhelmed, since the state of dissociation itself feels compromised— you feel like you've lost your brain. In severely dissociated state, you feel so disoriented and unable to focus that you don't realize you must put the milk in the refrigerator for storage.

Dissociation is a learned response to stress and threatening situations. There's no vote or conscious decision but an involuntary I'm outta here! Dissociation may last a few minutes or a few days, but some people spend most of their life in a severely dissociated state where they are numb to significant aspects of their life—most commonly their feelings, their body, or their environment.[5]

A confident, well-adjusted adult would gladly have taken their place at the "Big Table." They would have known that they had something to share or learn. My mental and emotional tabletop read "Abandoned." The legs supporting my tabletop were fear, prejudice, low self-esteem, and childhood emotional neglect or a low EQ (Emotional Intelligence).

Author Jasmin Cori writes about internal perpetrators:

While we all have an inner critic who pops up at times, those who were cruelly criticized while growing up often have an inner critic that is unnecessarily brutal. While it is sometimes believed that the inner critic is motivated by a positive intention of somehow protecting us (though in a very unskilled way), those with a history of abuse either have a critic gone wild or another part that is an inner perpetrator and often holds the same judgments as your abusive mother: You are no-good, fat, lazy, stupid, and should be exposed. Living with an internal perpetrator or even an out-of-control critic is hell. You are never safe from attack.[6]

I realized in that moment, on that phone call, Sue saw what I couldn't see in me. Sue saw character, integrity, intelligence, and a servant's heart. All I screamed to myself, using my inner voice, of course, was *they don't really like you, they are just being nice, and they just want what you can offer them.* The inner dialog continued, *No one really likes you. You can't compete with this crowd. They make more money than you. They are smarter than you. You are out of your league, girl. Shut up. Give them the card. Give them the card. Just give them the card!*

I wish I could say those were the only examples of how abandonment affected my wealth, but it wasn't.

MISSED OPPORTUNITIES

I am a gifted songwriter and play some guitar. If you give me a subject to write a song on, I probably can. So, people did. I sang at weddings and funerals and, of course, in church. I entered a few of my songs in contests, and they did well, coming in the top 100 to 300 out of thousands of entries. But the fear of singing in front of people caused me to try to sing like other artists, always thinking they were better. Yep, Imposter Syndrome once again. I remember singing Amy Grant songs over and over until I sounded just like her.

Low self-esteem and high pride go hand in hand, so trying to cover up for my low self-esteem, I would go into practice thinking I was Amy Grant. I remember clearly the day the worship leader said to me, "We already have an Amy Grant; that place is taken. However, we don't have a Rena, could we hear a little of her today?" I was devastated. Alone, I could sing loud and proud, but put me on a stage or with others I thought could sing better, and I just lost my voice. It would break, go flat, or just fail to come out. Would I ever stop performing and be an original? Even to this day I often can feel my throat tighten. I have battled asthma for as long as I can remember. I've had victory over it for as long as 11 years at a time. I notice that today, it only seems to show up when I am highly anointed and operating in my gift of the prophetic or when I am extremely anxious about something. I do not have the victory completely at the time of this writing, but my gloves are still on and I am still in the ring. I will be victorious.

One of the greatest compliments my husband ever gave me was when he announced we were going to have a radio program. I said, "What will we call it?" He said, "Heirloom Time." That was the title of one of the songs I wrote. He requested we use my song for the intro and outro of that radio program. We did it. The public loved it. It was free to use because I wrote it. My husband believed in me. But he's my husband—that's what husbands are supposed to do. Finally, without even trying, the radio listeners liked my voice and my song. I could feel my heart growing, but so was fear. Because the "What ifs?" started. What if they change their mind? What if they quit listening to the program? What if they leave you? "No!" I shouted. "Not this time. You are going to be okay. It is going to be okay."

I wrote many songs, but I never did much with any of them. One time I even heard a song on the radio much like the one I had written about three years earlier. I said, "Hey God, that's my song!" His answer was, "Yes, it was, but you failed to do it, so I gave it to someone else." It's the parable of the talents.[7] Songwriting was mine, but I buried it. I buried it out of fear. I missed my opportunity; one more sunrise I failed to see.

TIME TO CHANGE THE PATTERN

Not being a risk taker and believing the lie that you need the money before you can believe in yourself does not work. You must get some small wins under your belt. You must take your seat at the "Big Table." You and only you can change the trajectory of your worth and value. You are not your past or what happened to you.

I admit I am a work in progress. But I know my intellectual property is valuable. The information I have acquired getting to where I am today is valuable. The books I read were not free. The classes, the counseling, and the pain I have endured were all costly, but it is part of the tapestry of who I am today. Your tapestry may be like mine. On one side, it is a beautiful mosaic of your life that the world sees. The back of the tapestry may have some knots, some off pattern, unsightly and seemingly mishaps—but that is what it takes to get you from where you were, or still are, to where you are going and will one day be. So, embrace your originality; it is worth much more than a fake knockoff or a reproduction. Everyone wants an original, one-of-a-kind masterpiece. The world is waiting for people like you and me.

In *Healing for Damaged Emotions,* David Seamands writes:

> *It seems that God takes people with shortcomings and infirmities, gives them work to do, and then supplies them with sufficient grace to do it. Not many wise, not many noble, not many supermen, not many wonder women are on this team (1 Corinthians 1:26-31). The trouble is that low self-esteem robs God of marvelous opportunities to show off His power and ability through our weaknesses. Nothing sabotages Christian service more than thinking so little of yourself that you never really give God a chance. Are you in that picture? Freed, forgiven, a son, a daughter of God, a member of His family, but thinking of yourself as a worm or a grasshopper? Low self-esteem is Satan's deadliest psychological weapon, and it can keep you marching around in vicious circles of fear and uselessness.*[8]

It is time to cease marching to the rhythm of fear and uselessness. You are gifted. You can do it. God has called you, and the world awaits your gift. You are accepted. You may have a hard time believing it, but it is true. I believe in you—it is time for you to believe in yourself.

ENDNOTES

1. See Matthew 17:21-27.

2. Ed, Coambs. "How Childhood Trauma Can Impair Your Financial Well-Being." *Healthy Love & Money.* Posted July 28, 2022, on https://www.healthyloveandmoney. com/blog/how-childhood-trauma-can-impair-your-financial-well-being and retrieved on May 5, 2025.

3. Harter C.L., Harter J.F.R. "The Link Between Adverse Childhood Experiences and Financial Security in Adulthood." *J Fam Econ Issues.* 2022;43(4):832-842. doi: 10.1007/s10834-021-09796-y. Epub 2021 Sep 9. PMID: 34522076; PMCID: PMC8428486.

4. Elizabeth A., Waites. *Trauma and Survival, Trauma and Dissociative Disorders in Women* (New York: W.W. Norton and Company, 1993), 41.

5. Jasmin, Cori. *The Emotionally Absent Mother* (New York: The Experiment LLC, 2017), 123.

6. Ibid. 121.

7. See Matthew 25:14-30.

8. David, Seamands. *Healing Damaged Emotions.* (Colorado Springs: Life Journey. 2004). 54-55.

How Abandonment Affects Relationships

"The turning point in your relationship is the awareness that your growth is not about getting other people to change."

CLAUDIA BLACK

Abandonment affects all of us in some form or another. Perhaps you have not experienced it directly, and I genuinely hope that is the case. But chances are someone you are close to has experienced it to a degree, and what affects them affects you. There can even be family dynamics that carry forward as a result of childhood abandonment that happened three or four generations ago. If you are in relationships with people, I guarantee that abandonment issues play some role in them. If it hasn't already, it will. If it has, know that it doesn't have to continue.

I have been married for nearly fifty years to the same man. He has had to have a special grace to have a relationship with me. For years, I just held my breath, waiting for the day that he would abandon me too. It did not matter that he thought I was the most beautiful woman he had ever seen. He still believes it, and I have decided I am not going to argue with him! I just say, "Thank you, Honey." Then, I wink to myself internally and say *he must be blind—but then we all know that love is blind.*

He knows I have trust issues. I am the one that says, "Show me. Let me read it. Where did you get that information? Really? Seriously?" I am a person who insists, "That face was superimposed or glued on there, or AI did it." After all, if you can't trust your parents? Who can you trust? If you can't trust what was lived out in front of your very eyes—what you learned was all smoke and mirrors, then how well are you able to trust?

You don't.

You don't extend trust to anyone; it must be earned. Everyone must work to earn your trust, and even once they have earned it, they must occasionally prove it to you again. Some people find that offensive (and who can blame them). Others figure you are not worth the trouble. I mean, who wants to work their *entire life* getting you to trust them? Exactly. No one. But my husband has. He has been a gift to me. Regardless of all my scars, my issues, my insecurities, my illnesses, and near-death experiences. He has been the rock. My rock. He married into a family with abandonment issues that started long before I was even thought of.

In *Healing for Damaged Emotions*, David Seamands speaks of this phenomenon:

> *Who are the hardest people to get along with? Those who don't like themselves. Because they don't like themselves, they don't like others, and they're hard to get along with. Low self-esteem wrecks interpersonal relationships more than anything else I know.*
>
> *If you have low self-esteem, you ask another human being to do for you what no other person can do—to make you feel adequate and able—when you are already convinced that you are inadequate and unable. That is too heavy a demand on husband or wife, on children, friends, neighbors, or church. You may become either suspicious and hostile, or cringing and clinging ...*[1]

A PATTERN OF ABANDONMENT

Before I was born, actually before my grandmother was born, abandonment had already begun to do its devilish work in our family. In 1918, a deadly influenza pandemic, also known as the Spanish Flu, resulted in 50,000,000 people dying—two of which were my great-grandparents. They left behind six children, one of whom was my maternal grandmother. She was the youngest child and was later adopted. Grandma was abandoned by her parents when she was a little girl due to the death of her parents during that pandemic. There was no selfishness on the part of my great-grandparents; they did not *choose* to abandon her, but nevertheless, she was abandoned. Abandonment is not always because someone did someone or something wrong; sometimes traumatic or tragic things in life happen. We can feel as though we've been abandoned and still have our parents, our spouse, our boss, or whoever it is we feel has abandoned us.

It was difficult to map out our family tree, but our family members persevered, and we were able to find all the documents and learn that another family adopted my grandmother. She grew up, married, and had four children: three daughters and a son. When my mother was only four years old, on May 12, 1942, there was a mining explosion in our little hometown, resulting in the death of 56 miners, one of whom was my mother's daddy—my grandfather, who I would never get to meet.

Now, my grandmother was abandoned again, this time by her husband. She was left with four little children, no parents, and no spouse. I never met her because she died just a few weeks before I was born. This loss created abandonment for my mother right at the moment when she most needed emotional and physical support from her mom.

The trauma of abandonment and the tragedy of my grandmother's death threw my mother into early labor. She was medicated and hospitalized. As you have already learned, my mother felt overwhelmed, trapped, and unhappy, which led to her walking out on us, repeating the cycle of abandonment in our family. This real-life story shows three generations impacted by the abandonment of one or both parents. I am the fourth generation abandoned child.

Women are born with all the eggs they will ever have. So, when she carries a daughter, she also carries her grandchildren, as those girls are also born with all the eggs they will ever have. When my mother lost her mother, I was in her womb. Studies have shown that children in the womb feel sadness, stress, and other emotions of the mother. Sometimes, trauma is handed down, even though we may not know it. But often, and in my case, a traumatized parent raises traumatized children, who raise traumatized children. That does not even address ADHD and other mental issues that are inherited and handed down as well.

I don't know firsthand, but Daddy always brought up the story of when he brought me home from the hospital for the first time. I mentioned this in an earlier chapter, but it will make more sense now. My mother was abandoned by her daddy at four years old and now by her mother when she was just eighteen and pregnant with her first child. Oh, how that must have felt! Knowing your mother would never see your unborn child. She wouldn't be there to help you through labor or show you the ropes of early parenting. How do you nurse? Or will you bottle feed? Do I swaddle or not swaddle? How in the world do I bathe this little being? Knowing now what I have learned about dissociation, I don't think my mother was very involved with me as a newborn. I believe my father and paternal grandma helped—a lot. Perhaps even as an infant, I preferred Daddy. Maybe I sensed my mother's depression and distance. I don't know. I will never know.

I don't remember us ever being close. The only time I remember my mom brushing my hair was one Easter when I was five or six years old. She seemed rushed and agitated. I can assign words and language now to what I only felt as a child. I must have been squirming or not holding still; I can't recall. I do remember the sudden whack of the hairbrush on my head, the blood running warm down my face. I remember Mother opening the screen door onto the porch and how I ran to Daddy, who stooped down at the end of that driveway to receive me with open arms. I do remember the look he gave my mother. I do remember the trip to the Emergency Room—just Daddy and I—where I got stitches. I remember no other details. If my mother ever said anything about it, I have no memory of it. I also don't remember Daddy ever saying a word. It was the last time she hit me with a hairbrush—*that* I remember.

My next memory was this photo in my mind I can't erase. It was early in the morning. I had braids in my hair. My brother next to me looked about three years old, which would make me around seven years old. We are wrapped in a blanket on a metal glider on the front porch. I don't know where my mother was. Maybe she was asleep. Maybe she was getting ready for work. Maybe she was already at work. What matters is she wasn't there. Daddy scooped both my brother and me into his arms in one encompassing scoop and sat us in the front seat of his pickup truck. We were headed to Grandma's house. We both had chicken pox, I later learned, so we couldn't go to school. In my mind, it is another example of abandonment. We were sick, and Momma was nowhere to be found. But Daddy was there. Daddy was always there—until he wasn't.

Once we moved, it was baby after baby after baby—all boys. I remember Mom would call on the party line, and I would squeal, "Momma, what did you have? What was it? Did I get a sister? Did I?"

(Long pause.) "No honey, it's another boy."

"It's okay, Mom. You can bring him home, it's okay. Maybe next time."

The same scenario happened every year or so, and the answer was always the same. I never got that sister, but I do have one, even though I have never met her. She was conceived when my father was young and in the army in Germany. I have looked for her but have not found her as of the writing of this book. I am still looking.

When my fourth little brother was born, he was my real-life baby doll. My joy. Life seemed good. We watched *Hee Haw* together on our black-and-white TV. I would run and turn the antenna. We would all sneak and watch *Chiller Theatre* and scare ourselves to death. We rode bikes. We worked in the garden. We did our chores. We played in the rain, in the snow, in the leaves, and in the hot summer sun with no sunscreen. We even went camping, fishing, and skinny dipping with Ivory Soap to take our baths because it was white and floated. Those were the good years, or so I thought. I never knew a storm was brewing. I had no idea that one day in my future, I would become co-dependent for fear of being abandoned. I didn't know that the wounded child in me would take charge of my adult emotions.

> I didn't know the wounded child in me would take charge of my adult emotions.

John Bradshaw describes it in this way:

> *The disease of my disease was the insatiable wounded child that ruled my life. I had to experience that child's pain. My belief is that all of us who identify ourselves as co-dependent will have to go through some kind of grief process if we want to be free of our compulsivity. When we are in touch with our true feelings, the energy to act them out is gone.*[2]

So, today, even when things are going great, I'm anxious. I am sometimes afraid that something bad is happening, and I am just not observing it. Surely, I'm missing something. What isn't being said? Are there looks being shared I don't see? So, I feel jumpy in relationships, unpredictable in how to respond, and untrusting in what I see and feel.

In my relationships, I struggle to trust. I always wonder if others have an agenda. Are they telling me the truth? Do they really love me? Will they always love me? When I was little, I couldn't articulate these feelings. I had no vocabulary to express emotions. I didn't have a Plutchik Wheel with the eight core emotions and their opposites: joy—sadness, trust—disgust, fear—anger, surprise—anticipation to help me explain.[3] I had no feeling chart with smiley and frowny faces like they now use to teach children how to identify and describe their emotions. I can only imagine how helpful it would have been to circle the face of how I was feeling so someone would understand! Basically, as an adult with abandonment issues, my emotions do not fit one category on the wheel. My wheel goes round and round. "Tell me what you want me to be, and I will be it." That was my life.

BOUNDARIES, SELF-AWARENESS, AND ROLES WE PLAY

I had no boundaries. I did not know where I ended and others began. I did not know in what role I was cast. In my marriage, I would become a mother when I felt out of control or afraid instead of the trusting wife I was supposed to be. When insecurity arose, I would immediately go into protection mode even if others or myself did not need to be protected. I spent years confused. Overstepping my boundaries was common. *What boundary? I didn't see that boundary.* I did some really dumb things, like take control of the thermostat because I would see people shivering or getting their coats on and it wasn't even my meeting. Now, that will hurt a relationship or chance of promotion. Once, I gave someone permission to handle something, but I had not been given any authority or responsibility to tell anyone to do anything. I did not want to be in a relationship with myself, let alone anyone else. I was always stepping over boundaries and didn't begin to know how to make a boundary or that I could even set a boundary. I worked for hours for one person who never paid me, or for that matter, was ever really pleased with the best I could give. They just kept demanding more from me.

I have learned a great deal about boundaries in recent years, and one of the best resources has been Dr. Henry Cloud. In his book *Changes That Heal,* he writes:

> *Many people struggle to discover, set, and guard their personal boundaries. They truly cannot tell where they end and someone else begins, and thus suffer from lack of purpose, powerlessness, panic, identity loss, eating disorders, depression, irresponsibility, and a whole host of other*

problems, all of which lead to a lack of real intimacy with others.

Probably the most destructive result of lack of boundaries is physical and emotional abuse. People who are unable to set boundaries allow themselves to be repeatedly controlled and even injured by others.[4]

Being self-aware and self-compassionate are not easy for me. I learned early to be responsible for my little brothers. If someone got hurt, it was always, "You should have been watching him." I am an expert at "other aware" as opposed to being self-aware. Then, I go into the fix-it mode. I bark out orders and shout directions. If I think I am not being heard, I raise my voice louder. I then start repeating the same thing over and over again. I began to realize that I was like a chameleon. Be whatever you need to be at the moment. Do what was needed to bring peace and stability to chaos. I would adjust my behavior to match any situation that arose. One minute, I was a responsible little adult who did everything right and figured out that if I didn't do it, well, it would not get done. Then, I would adjust when Dad would remarry and take the back seat. I just figured that to get along, I needed to go along, or God forbid, the stepmother would leave too.

When reading the book *Changing Course* by Claudia Black, I realized that I didn't know who I was. I had no idea how to have a relationship with anyone because all I knew from my survival skills was how to identify myself based on where I'd come from and lived through. I learned that being dysfunctional was not because I was bad, wrong, or flawed. I did not know how to have a healthy relationship because I wasn't healthy mentally. I grew up in a dysfunctional family. I had experienced abandonment.

Claudia Black, a well-known author and lecturer, writes:

> As people move into adulthood, they take with them the identity of their family role. A person who had been the Responsible Child will most often continue to demonstrate that role in adult relationships by being a leader and being goal-oriented.[5]

Black goes on to describe four roles that children adapt to when growing up in a dysfunctional family where loss, fear, and abandonment are the running themes within the family system. She describes the four roles as follows:

- **The Responsible Child:** *Being the proverbial family leader. The strengths identified are as follows: Well-organized, leadership skills, decision-maker, initiator, perfectionist, and goal-oriented. There are weaknesses: Inflexibility, need to be right, severe need to be in control, and the list goes on. A brief would be, "If I don't do it, no one will."*

- ***The Adjuster Child:*** *They still need someone else to provide structure for them to react: Some of their strengths are ability to follow, flexibility, and follows without asking questions. Their deficits include fear of making a mistake, lack of direction inability to perceive options power. A belief would be, "If I don't get emotionally involved, I won't get hurt."*

- ***Placater Child:*** *The placater continues in adulthood to take care of the emotional needs within the family system. Their strengths include caring, empathetic, sensitive to others, and a good listener. Their deficits identified are an inability to receive, guilty, and a strong fear of anger. A brief would be, "If I am nice, people will like me."*

- ***The Acting Out Child:*** *These children are the ones most apt to have experienced some form of direct intervention. These people are often in trouble with society in their young adulthood. Their strengths include close to their own feelings, less denial and greater honesty, creative, and having a sense of humor. Their deficits are an inappropriate expression of anger, inability to follow directions, and intrusive. A brief would be, "If I scream loudly enough, someone may notice me."*[6]

No wonder those closest to me have had it the toughest. I don't share this abandoned person called "me" with everyone. They do not get the "Acting Out Child." Everyone else gets the "Responsible Child," the performer, the perfectionist, the calm, cool, and collected actress who wonders how long she can keep it up ... and *when, oh, when can I go home and take a nap?* Those closest to me get the real me. Mask off, guard down, exhausted, disappointed, discouraged, depressed, want to throw in the towel "Acting Out" me. Not fair. Not loving. Not a fruit that others can taste and see that God is good. As I write this, it seems ages ago that it was me this all happened to, who went through these events—but it was me. I am so grateful to have been given the time on this earth to figure some things out, heal, understand, and share my journey.

> The life I live now is a life of challenges, changes, and chances that I am willing to take to become the person I was always created to be.

The life I live now is a life of challenges, changes, and chances that I am willing to take to become the person I was always created to be. Free. No longer a child but an adult that can stay in her adult chair and not succumb to sitting in her child chair trying to keep the world from falling apart. There comes a time in all of our lives when we must choose to take responsibility for our own actions and stop blaming our past but learn from it.

*"Everyone wanted me to feed them that story—
darkness to light, weakness to strength, broken to
whole. I wanted it, too."*

— JOHN GREEN, *TURTLES ALL THE WAY DOWN*

As a young Christian, I remember my pastor calling me into her office and sharing with me that I needed to try harder because most of the women in the church didn't like me. Her words were, "They think that you think you're too good for them. That you are a snob. That you are stuck up." I wanted to cry. I'm sure my face showed it. She was the greatest pastor ever and remains so at this writing. I tried to explain that with my low self-esteem, I was trying my best to be accepted. I never realized I was over-compensating, and it appeared as high pride. She agreed that I may have felt insecure and unprepared, less than unworthy, but that's not at all how it came across. She prayed for me that I could begin to learn how to be me and show myself friendly. The only problem was the real me was truly too friendly. I complimented others often. I told them they were pretty. I made friends quickly. I remembered their special occasions and birthdays; I became what I was looking for, and that didn't work either. Fear and shame were always talking to me from the inside, and then on the outside, I heard things like, "She's too nice. No one is that nice." I felt like I wore a sign around my neck that read, "It's okay to abandon me; go ahead. I'm used to it."

Claudia Black shares:

When you no longer operate from a basis of fear and shame, you can more easily let go of childhood family rules and roles. When you do, you will find a freedom in relationships not previously experienced.[7]

Since my mother left when I was young, I really didn't know a thing about raising young girls to be young women. I was a great mom when they were babies, but as they got older, all I knew how to do was work and make money and buy them what they wanted. So, I did. Then, we had a house fire, and all their possessions, including the hermit crab, were gone. I spent an entire year finding the storybooks I had read to them when they were little. I searched eBay to find all the Strawberry Shortcake characters and scanned the flea markets for the beloved childhood Berenstein Bear books that were their favorites. Christmas came, and I had been receiving packages from across the United States for months. But, when all the gifts were opened, I could tell I had missed it. They didn't want what they had. I wanted to replace what they had. Hear what I just said, "I wanted to replace what they had." I wasn't healed of my own loss.

I never asked *them* what *they* wanted. Why? I was never asked what I wanted. I always made a list and my parents did a great job just buying what was on the list. I missed it. To this day, I am just figuring things out. Here's a help list:

Our children are not a little version of us. They are not a "Lil' Me." They are their own person. They did not live your trauma. Your children didn't have your parents for a parent. Their brains are wired differently than yours.

Times have changed. Don't buy them what you want them to have. Purchase for them what they desire (within reason). Ask them questions. Listen to their answers.

Dr. Henry Cloud writes:

> We learn how the world is and adapt to it. We construct a map of relationship, and how it works. The problem is that we may construct our map in a hurtful setting, and then, when we are older and out of that setting, we forget to update it. Our twenty-year-old map then becomes a barrier to living fully, to relating to others.[8]

My map in adulthood was constructed in early adolescence. There was no way that map was going to navigate adulthood, marriage, children, church leadership, and all the other plates I needed to keep spinning. Then, I would feel guilty for dropping a plate. Dr. Henry Cloud talks about how feelings of guilt have their roots in a lack of bonding, and he is right: it is a vicious cycle. I know that lack well.

CYCLES REPEAT UNLESS WE BREAK THEM

I just shared about our house fire in 1994 where we lost everything. Once again, I felt abandoned—only this time by God. My children lost everything. I didn't know what questions to ask my children after the fire. I was afraid of bringing up bad memories, so I didn't talk about the fire with them. I wanted them to forget it happened. So, I decided early on not to bring it up. Later, much later, my adult children said to me, "Mom, you never let us process the losses we experienced after our house fire. You never let us go through the scene of the fire afterward and see it for ourselves. You never sent us to therapy." Truth be known, in 1994, no one I knew of sent their kid to therapy.

It's true, though. I should have found a counselor or therapist for them to talk to. My dad should have gotten all five of us therapy when our mother left. We should have been able to process the events. I did what was modeled for me. I ignored it, but ignoring things doesn't make them go away. It does not fix them or heal our souls. It just keeps the cycle going.

Lesson learned.

My parents never came to anything I ever did at school. I understand now it was because they worked. Other parents came, so I couldn't understand it at that time. I wanted my parents to be there, but it seemed they always had an excuse. I was even the head majorette and had a parade at Christmas, and I wanted them to be there. They weren't.

I was a cheerleader in high school, and Mom was gone by then. So, I wanted Daddy there. He never came. But, when my brother started playing football, Dad never missed a game. I wondered why there were different rules for girls and boys. It only enforced the lie that I believed I should have been a boy and that I didn't matter. I have since come to terms with the fact that I am not a disappointment. I am *exactly* who God intended me to be. I am a woman born for the times in which we live. I am not perfect, but I am a child of God, and He loves me. I refuse to base my happiness on my gender. I love being a woman. I love being a mother, and a wife, and a grandmother. If you look for the good, you will find it. If you look for what is wrong—you will find that too.

> *"You are your own worst enemy. If you can learn to stop expecting impossible perfection, in yourself and others, you may find the happiness that has always eluded you."*
>
> — LISA KLEYPAS, *LOVE IN THE AFTERNOON*

Adults often have no idea the impact they have on the future adult version of children.

Adults often have no idea the impact they have on the future adult version of children. By my senior year of high school, the secret was out: my parents were divorced. I was the only kid in my school whose parents were divorced. In 1973 and 1974, where I lived, it was unheard of for a man to raise his children alone. When the teachers all found out, things changed. I was a great cheerleader, but I wasn't chosen for the squad. The reason—I had no mother. Who would get my uniform ready? Who would take me and bring me to the games? Did they not know I could do all that myself—even better than some mothers? Guess not. So, in my senior year, I went from being a somebody to a nobody.

I should have known something bad would happen. Good things never last, right? People don't really care about other people; they just look out for themselves. That was almost fifty years ago, and I am still competing in marathons and am in as good of shape, maybe better than I was before having three kids. My cheerleading mother saw me a few years back and couldn't believe how well I turned out. She was, to say the least, surprised—well, I think it was more shock and awe.

I wasn't the greatest at letting my children go. I wanted them to be my children forever, but that's not how it's supposed to be. I wish someone would have told me I was raising daughters that would grow up and have jobs, raise families, pay bills, and go on vacations with their families. That they would love God and serve Him. That they would love me, but they would leave me—not abandon me, but leave as they should—and one day be my friends. I would have done things differently. But no one told me. No one taught me. I didn't know.

But now I have learned.

Today I have one daughter who has invested her life in helping other children. She has her master's degree in social work and makes a difference every day in the lives of children less fortunate from troubled homes and addicted parents. She is my hero.

My other daughter is married and has adopted two boys and given birth to my only granddaughter. She cooks, cleans, and makes sure her children have all their needs and wants met. She gets them any kind of intervention or therapy they need. She, too, is my hero.

I still have friends from over 45 years ago. We may not see one another often, but we pick up right where we left off. They were my models, and I was theirs. Though we never knew how much we needed each other. They are still my heroes, and I am theirs. For years, we called one another "The Steels." Unfortunately, some of those relationships have abandoned me, too. Differences of opinion and lifestyles caused us to drift apart or be torn apart. Times change, I tell myself. It's okay. Honestly, today in my journey—it is okay.

In *The DNA of Relationships*, Gary Smalley writes:

> *Relationships are **not** optional. From the moment we're born, we're in relationship with parents, siblings, and other relatives. Soon, we're in relationship with other children. Later, we have relationships at school and in the workplace, and we develop relationships with close friends.*

Eventually, most people develop a relationship with someone they deeply love.

When a relationship becomes difficult or painful, we tend to dismiss the relationship and may, for a while, try to abandon all relationships. But inevitably, we come back and seek connection again.

Though we can choose how we will participate in relationships, we have no choice about whether we will participate in them. This is a critical point. Our only real choice is whether we will work to make our relationships healthy; whether we will do things that hinder or enhance them.

Dr. Dean Ornish has found in his research that "loneliness and isolation ... increase the likelihood of disease and premature death from all causes by 200 to 500 percent or more... In short, anything that promotes a sense of isolation often leads to illness and suffering. Anything that promotes a sense of love and intimacy, connection, and community is healing.[9]

I have a church and network of pastors that I model being a mother to. Seems strange the one thing I didn't have, I am and am able to give to others. I cheer for their victories. I believe in their dreams. I confront their hindrances and help them to see their giftings and callings. I openly share my hopes, dreams, and fears for them. I hold them in my heart real hard, but in my hands openly, so they know they can fly—in fact, so they can soar.

> *"Expectations were like fine pottery. The harder you held them, the more likely they were to crack."*
>
> — BRANDON SANDERSON, *THE WAY OF KINGS*

At the heart of every struggle with abandonment lies a sacred longing—to know that we are not alone. The wounds left by early disconnection echo through all our relationships, shaping how we love, trust, and protect ourselves. But there is an invitation for us to awaken, and when we become aware and recognize destructive patterns, we can interrupt them instead of repeating them. The inability to feel or express emotions, the broken boundaries, and the generational echoes of loss are not the end of our story. When we bring compassion to the wounded child within, we begin the holy work of transformation.

Healing is not a return to what was … it looks a lot more like growing into what can be …

Trust can be rebuilt.

Established boundaries can bring blessings.

Love—real, whole, and rooted in our God-given identity—can allow us to be fully seen and fully known without fear of abandonment.

Healing is not a return to what was. You will never replace what was missing or absent from your life. Healing looks a lot more like growing into what can be, guided by grace, intention, and the quiet wisdom of a restored soul.

ENDNOTES

1. David, Seamands. *Healing for Damaged Emotions,* (Colorado Springs, CO: Life Journey-Cook Communications Ministries 2004), 53.

2. John, Bradshaw. *Bradshaw On: The Family,* (Deerfield Beach, FL.: Health Communications Inc. 1996), 231.

3. Plutchik's Wheel of Emotions was developed in 1980 by Robert Plutchik, Ph.D. illustrate different emotions.

4. Henry, Cloud. *Changes that Heal,* (St. Rapids, MI: Zondervan Publishing 1990), 111.

5. Claudia, Black. *Changing Course, Healing from Loss, Abandonment, and Fear,* (Center City: Hazelden Publishing 1999), 120-122.

6. Ibid.

7. Ibid, p.131.

8. Henry, Cloud. *Changes that Heal,* (St. Rapids, MI: Zondervan Publishing 1990), 85.

9. Gary, Smalley. *The DNA of Relationships,* (Carol Stream, IL: Tyndale House Publishers, Inc. 2007), *12.*

The Fear of Loss and Disappointments

"When you're born in a burning house, you think the whole world is on fire. But it's not."

RICHARD KADREY

In one of the greatest anthologies ever written, there is a book called Job. I am referring, of course, to the Bible. The Book of Job is a profound story that explores the nature of suffering, loss, disappointment, grief, justice, and divine sovereignty. In it, we find that the main character, Job, experiences his greatest fears coming upon him. He lost his wealth, his children, and his health. Interestingly, Job did nothing to bring these circumstances about—the losses were not consequences of his bad decisions or actions. He was an upright man who was tested and tormented by Satan. Though

Job wrestled with the injustice of his plight, he maintained a steadfast hope in God, who responded with a powerful declaration of divine wisdom and pointed out the limits of human understanding. When Job humbly accepts this, the Lord restores to him all that he had and more. Job received twice the wealth he previously had and was given seven sons and three daughters.

While this sounds like a happy ending, I confess that this never totally comforted me because I don't believe one child can replace another. The loss is permanent, even if another child arrives as a blessing.

LOSING A CHILD

On March 31, 1980, I gave birth to my first child. A beautiful baby girl. She lived inside me for more than eight months, but she lived outside my womb for just sixteen days and had to endure five surgeries. There's something very special about bringing forth life. Then, when something goes wrong, the weight of disappointment is overwhelming. Losing a child in no way compares to the loss and abandonment I had experienced from my mother and father. The loss of a child is one of the greatest losses I believe a mother can experience. It was years before I could share my experiences surrounding her life. Today, she would be 45 years old. I often wonder what occupation she would have chosen. Would she have married and had children? These are questions I know will never be answered. I can't imagine what it would be like to spend time with her. I do, however, remember every day without her.

> *Fear of abandonment is not a clinical diagnosis in and of itself. It is a form of anxiety and a symptom of several clinical disorders, including both mood and personality disorders. Individuals who experience abandonment are also more likely to have long-term mental health issues.[1]*

Being an avid reader and noticing how themes in life keep coming up when we are going through a difficult time, I read the book *Beyond Words: What Animals Think and Feel* by Carl Safina. In it, he talks about how when a female elephant gives birth to a stillborn baby, she will stay with her dead child for four days, carrying it around all alone in the heat, guarding it from lions. He pointed out that the mothers never carry healthy calves. He shares that grief isn't only a response to death. We can also grieve for living people who have walked out of our lives. He says, "Knowing them changed our lives, and losing them changes our lives."

Profound.

With the death and loss of my first child, I was forever changed. I remain changed even now. I'm not mad at God. I'm not mad at all. My heart still hurts, though, and the loss remains. The hard thing for me to admit is that my fear of abandonment was reinforced in me as her death left a void in my life that seemingly nothing could fill. The doctors emphasized that her death was not from anything we did or didn't do. It was not chromosomal. It was not because of her DNA; it was just a very rare and unusual birth defect that involved her heart.

When she died, I was lost, caught up in grief, loss, and confusion as to why it happened. Fear and abandonment were reinforced, and I believe this contributed to my despair.

In *Helping Children Cope With Separation and Loss,* Claudia Jarratt writes:

> *Despair is perhaps the most difficult stage of grief to experience or to witness. The bereaved person sinks into a bleak, hopeless state of mind that resembles clinical depression. A child in despair may speak and move more slowly, seem pessimistically resigned to the interest in eating, grooming, and socializing diminishes sharply. The child feels helpless and hopeless: it seems as if the worst possible thing that could happen has happened. Life seems both meaningless and overwhelming. Why get up? Why go to bed? Why eat? Why care?[2]*

At the young age of twenty-four, I thought my world had ended. I was left again—abandoned—to grieve alone except for my husband, my father-in-law, and my mother. This time, I don't remember my father being there for me. He was now married to my stepmother, and she had turned all of his attention to her children and away from the five of us. There were years I felt as though I no longer existed to my father. It was so painful living with my stepmother that I moved out as a senior in high school and lived on the campus at WVU with five other girls. My father emotionally and physically abandoned me. My mother came to the funeral. She was late, and on the advice of the funeral director, the casket was already closed, so she never saw my daughter. The funeral home refused to leave it open for the funeral ceremony because we had allowed a total autopsy to be completed, and they felt it would be too hard on my husband and me and our families because babies just look like they are sleeping. They also requested she wear a bonnet. We were young and just did what we were told.

If I could do it over, I would have taken pictures while she was in the hospital and even in the casket. Everyone told me no, wait till you take her home. The problem was I never got to bring her home. So I have not one photo of my beautiful dark-haired baby girl, but I still remember what she looked like. I remember her cry and her fighting spirit. She was able to convince the most talented and committed surgeons that she was going to make it. She showed me fight. She showed me, "I want to stay with you, Mom. I'm doing everything I can to live." Today, as a pastor and a friend, when this type of trauma occurs in our congregation or among friends, I encourage them to take photos. Take as many as you want. I will take them for you. I realize now my daughters would love to see what their older sister looked like. One more go-along-to-get-along-don't-rock-the-boat decision I wish I had never made. I wish I would have been brave and told them what I wanted.

Her loss was a tragic time in our young life and marriage. We slept a lot. People didn't know what to say, so most said nothing. It's strange how when you lose someone you love, you want the world to stop—but it goes on. I was thrown deeper into grief, also a word I was unfamiliar with. The disappointment of coming home to an empty nursery was gut-wrenching. I did not want to put her little coffin in the cold ground. The day we buried her, it snowed. I just wanted to bring her home.

Claudia Jarratt observes:

> *Early disappointment is a factor that sets the stage for one kind of double or dissociated existence. Following disappointment, the individual's inner work is often divided into before and after. Before can be idealized as a golden age when things were going well. After is like life for Adam and Eve after the Fall—a time of pain and gloom and isolation from good feelings. To the extent that everybody experiences disappointments, everybody understands such mythic images as that of the golden age. Abused children, however, experience unusually intense disappointment, and coping with disappointment is complicated by coping with the effects of abuse ...[3]*

LOSING A SIBLING

I unknowingly lived my entire life in grief. I had lost love. I had lost the love of a mother, a father, and now a daughter. Shortly thereafter, my youngest brother (my baby) died in a motorcycle accident at the tender age of nineteen on September 11, 1982. Once again, Claudia Jarratt's words hit home:

> *Children who lose a sibling suffer massive changes.*
> *They may become only children; they may become*
> *the oldest and feel an extra burden of responsibility*
> *as a result. They have lost a playmate, companion,*
> *and rival, and all the familiar interactions and*
> *expectations that were connected to those*
> *relationships.[4]*

I was always the responsible child, and I stepped into the role again, helping my father handle all the details of my brother's death. I can't possibly include all the losses here of loved ones who were gone too soon: my grandparents, who were like parents to me; my stepfather, who always said, "There are NO stepchildren, only children," and loved me as his own, and so many more. They left my life, and each time, those feelings of abandonment, loss, grief, and disappointment resurfaced with a vengeance. The snowball of abandonment was picking up power and speed from generations back. This time that snowball knocked my door down. Mother never said, "I love you, bye." I never got to say,

"Love you, bye" to my baby brother, and I never got to say "I love you, bye" to my little girl. To this day, it is very important to me when someone leaves that they say, "Love you, bye." It is also very important to me to do the same. I unconsciously or maybe consciously want closure.

On the subject of the importance of closure to healing, Jarratt writes:

> After the news of the upcoming loss or change has been introduced and explored, children need to be given the opportunity to say whatever good-byes are involved. Having the chance to say actual thought-out good-byes to people, places, or familiar family structures is among the most healing things a child can experience. Not only do such good-byes give the child a chance to review and acknowledge the good things that will be lost, they also allow the child an opportunity to express those feelings face-to-face with others who are involved. A thoughtful good-bye visit leaves less unfinished business to complicate the grief that follows the loss. Youngsters who do not have the chance to exchange good-byes or to receive permission to move on sometimes are more likely to sustain additional damage to their basic sense of trust and security additional damage to their basic sense of trust and security, to their self-

esteem, and to their ability to initiate and sustain
strong relationships as they grow up.[5]

This is the very reason I am known for always saying, "Love you, bye." I say it at the end of every phone call, every visit, when we leave church, a friend's house, or a gathering. Many of my closest friends give me a big smile and the look when they teasingly say, "Love you, bye." It wasn't until I wrote this book that it all made sense. I never got to say or hear those words.

LOSS THROUGH THE LENS
OF ABANDONMENT

Everyone experiences loss and disappointment. But when you have been abandoned, these things impact you differently. You are more likely to see a loss or disappointment as a personal rejection, even when it is not intended that way. You may seek to avoid the pain of loss through unhealthy coping mechanisms or react with such intense emotions that it feels disproportionate to the situation. While it is natural to grieve loss and disappointment for those with abandonment issues, rather than processing grief in healthy stages, it is easy to get stuck in unhealthy patterns of denial, anger, despair, or avoidance.

Those who have been victims of or experienced abandonment may look like everyone else on the outside— healthy, successful, and resilient. Abandonment issues are not always obvious. For the most part, we seem like everyone else, but we are hiding a lot underneath our performance, our addictions to food, drugs, alcohol, or spending, etc. We try to work for love, buy love, and perform for love, but nothing fills the unseen void.

Those of us with abandonment issues cause some of our own losses and disappointments because we unwittingly sabotage relationships. Many with abandonment issues fail to form lasting relationships, which has nothing to do with bad fortune. It has to do with fear of loss and fear of disappointment. However, as in my own life, I can expect too much and then get disappointed. I often feel powerless, and that causes me to have push-pull, yes-no, in relationships, and so I create my own abandonment cycle over and over.

As a woman who was abandoned, I live in fear of my embarrassing, self-defeating, and destructive behavior being exposed. I find my self-dialogue often shouting, "What if?" In my experience, if abandonment issues are ignored and allowed to linger way too long, they start to affect all the other areas in our life. Throughout my adulthood, I have grappled with: *What is wrong with me? Why do I act the way I do?* I have probably read

> **If abandonment issues are ignored and allowed to linger way too long, they start to affect all the other areas in our life.**

more self-help books than I could ever possibly name. My shelves are over-filled—I own eight very large bookshelves in my home, not including rooms full of bookshelves in my pastoral library and my office at home and at work. Yet, I remained confident in my outside world performance while my inside world was crumbling. I kept striving for acceptance, recognition, attention, love, and affirmation like a small child, like an abandoned child. That's where I got off—as a child. It showed up when I least expected it. It showed up as anxiety. It showed up as depression. It showed up when I could no longer cover it up as undiagnosed ADHD. Fear follows you when you expect it to. Disappointment means we had an expectation. So, my childlike solution was to quit expecting.

Once, for a small stint, I worked for my husband. We owned a pre-owned automobile business for many years. He was headed out of the country, so I volunteered to run the business. After a conversational training that went something like this, "Just get the money; I will figure out everything else when I get home," he left me and our two young daughters and headed across the ocean, fulfilling the call of God on his life. Okay, easy enough. Get the money. I sold a car a day for five days straight, and I got the money! I even sold a car to someone who didn't even have a license. It turns out you don't need a license to purchase a car—but you need one to drive it off the lot! I just didn't know what I didn't know.

While my husband was gone that week, my dad stopped by to visit. We had one other person in the office. I was thrilled to see my dad. He stayed awhile and then left. After his departure, the gentleman who worked for us said, "I can't understand you."

"Excuse me? What don't you understand?" I asked.

"Your dad walks in, and the beautiful, confident, successful woman I know and admire turns into a thirteen-year-old girl," he said.

And he was right.

He didn't know my past. He had no idea, but there it was again. I was exposed. I was embarrassed. What I tried so hard to keep the world from seeing was showing up again. It was like seeing the red all over again, that everyone else knew about but I was blind to, not privy to, until my teacher had taken me aside that day. After my dad left, I rehearsed the visit in a microwave minute. I did change. I did perform. But I would not fully understand why for many more years filled with similar incidences. With each incident came more embarrassment, greater fear of what I didn't know, of just being myself in front of others. If our employee could see the abandoned, childhood emotionally neglected little girl in a short visit with her father, who else knew? I had to do better. I had to try harder. I had to learn more. It wouldn't be until many years later that the epiphany would have me writing this book. I composed it on my office floor with tears of loss and disappointment long before this pen touched paper and my fingers braved the keys of my laptop.

No longer did I fear just disappointing others, now the fear had grown into a silent terror. The anxiety of that day could not be erased. The words were spoken. In my mind, I had disappointed my employee. I had lost control, and I must remain in control at all times. This took the form of extreme weight loss. It was something I could control. Allow me to explain ...

EXERTING CONTROL TO MASK FEAR OF EXPOSURE

Let's rewind to that house fire—another loss and a huge disappointment. Fortunately, we had insurance. It wasn't our fault. A nail through a wire in the ceiling had acted over the years as a type of kindling, and the house went up in a swirling inferno. Fortunately, we owned property where the car lot was located, and above the office was a small one-room apartment. This served as our home for 365 days to the day. Two daughters, one teenage and one about to be, one cat, one dog, and the two of us. Looking back, I can barely believe we survived that year. I went for a lot of walks with my dog, then with my girls to the local pool, and then another one in the evening with my husband.

On one of these walks, I got lost and found the house we now call home. Funny how when you are lost, you often find what you are looking for. I am a Christian, and sometimes the Lord talks to me. So, on this walk, I clearly heard, "This is your house," and it has now been our home for over 31 years. However, for an entire year, we had no place to call home, we were living in one room, and I felt abandoned by God. The loss of all my belongings was overwhelming to me and my girls. I would go to get something, knowing I had it, and then realize, "Oh, it was burnt in the fire." Disappointment over precious items ripped away by the flames I couldn't quench seemed to burn hotter some days even though the house was long gone. I had emotion attached to that home. It was the place I brought my babies home to. It was the place where we had our first puppy, our first kitten, our first birthdays—so many firsts.

I still vividly recall details about the fire. The smell. The clothes I wore. I remember where I was when I got the call. It's weird how abandonment can steal some memories and yet forever etch in your mind the ones you would like to forget. That very night, my husband and I were at a friend's wedding rehearsal. I'm sure we smelled like smoke. Nowhere to shower. No time to change. Ironically, the bridesmaids didn't carry flowers; we had to carry lanterns. Lit lanterns. Real flames! This was a huge trigger for me.

> It's weird how abandonment can steal some memories and yet forever etch in your mind the ones you would like to forget.

When we moved out of the one-room apartment above the car lot, we moved into a large four-bedroom home. The cat and dog ran up and down the stairs and from room to room. The girls picked their rooms, and for a while, the echo of emptiness was haunting to me. It reminded me of the eerie silence of that day I came home from school to find Momma's letter. No furniture, no pictures on the walls, no rugs on the floor, just an empty house. Much like a room in my empty heart. The echo of my longing for acceptance, for my mother's love, my father's unconditional presence— unbeknownst to me, that acceptance from them would never come, or at least not the way I thought it would. Loss and disappointment became my constant companion.

We got busy cleaning the house we were moving into. I stayed up until the wee hours of the morning trying to make that big house our home. We began to pull up carpet, wash down walls, and empty a box truck of the few items salvaged from the basement and garage of our old house. An olfactory memory overwhelmed me as we took each item from the box truck. I found the only cleaning agent that worked was "Mean Green." I was allergic to it. With the hard work, no sleep, and the allergic reactions combined, my weight dropped drastically. With the weight loss, however, I felt empowered. It seemed that people couldn't see that thirteen-year-old girl anymore. All they saw was skinny, so I kept getting thinner. It got me attention. It worked for a few years until I got a job teaching aerobics. Then, it went to working out three times a day. Friends who hadn't seen me for a while didn't seem to notice anything but the new skinnier, stronger me. Loss and disappointment were covered up with how I looked. My abandonment was disguised.

With a new home and the updates, cleaning, and making the house a home, I think I felt better than I had in years. Once settled, I started spinning all the plates again. I couldn't go through the pictures from the fire for over 20 years. I just kept putting off the inevitable boxes of burned photo albums and pictures. Procrastination always came up surrounding the photos. I think back, and I realize I just couldn't. When it was time, I finally tackled it with the help of my husband's organizational gift and direction. By this time, the girls were grown. So, they each got their very own tote of photos. As I looked through the tattered, burned, crumbled photos, a wave of loss came over me again. *Where did all those years go? Do the girls even remember the trips to Disney, birthday parties, dance recitals, ball games, track meets, and performances?* I was such a perfectionist, driving, running late, last-minute rushing, everything-has-to-be-just-right mom; I realize I took a lot of fun out of their younger years. Because I came from workaholic parents, I became a workaholic. Due to the years of pushing, I had gotten on that hamster wheel and never knew how to get off—until I fell off. Looking back, I can't help but be disappointed we didn't have more fun. Sure, we made memories—but I can't remember them. I made them tasks and checked them off my list. I guess I didn't want them to miss anything. I wanted them to do things and go places with me, but I didn't know how to "be" with them—just be. I never paused to really get to know my children's little personalities and learn how to blend mine with theirs.

Claudia Jarratt remarks:

> *Some children become prematurely competent or self-reliant as a way of keeping themselves safe. Perhaps their attempts to make and maintain satisfying, positive relationships or to reestablish connections have been unsuccessful, and they come to believe that reaching out, getting close to, or depending on others is too hurtful and disappointing to risk.*[6]

GROWING HEALTHY AND EMBRACING CHANGE

Today, I have another chance. I do things differently with my grandchildren, and I am totally present. I am not focused on what people think or if the house is clean (although it usually is), I am able to just be. I can be present watching TV about princesses or animals repeatedly—it doesn't bother me a bit. I snuggle into that blanket and get all cozy right with them. I also try my best to be there for my grown daughters, even though, at times, their independence and upbringing do not allow for free time for them to play. I understand why. I take full responsibility for how I raised them. I have learned that you can't unspill spilled milk. But we do not have to walk around in the milk; we can clean it up and move on.

So, you see, with abandonment comes a lot of fear of loss and disappointment. Many of us set ourselves up for these.

We don't know how to stop the fears and disappointments. We must learn what we missed learning when we experienced childhood emotional neglect, were abandoned, and disappointed as children.

We carry with us the losses and disappointments that everyone else does, but they are like being on steroids. We feel the colors of abandonment and loss; we don't just respond to them—we react. It takes a lot of patience with yourself and sharing with those closest that you need their help. I often ask people to say things calmly and nicely so I cannot just hear what they are saying, but remember what they say. I remind them if they are edgy and raise their voice, I will not remember what they said. I try very hard not to tune them out and go numb. Today, I win more days than I lose or get disappointed.

In *Trauma and Survival,* Elizabeth Waites writes:

> *Once love has evolved, the individual sometimes fears psychological loss more than physical destruction. The fear of loss then leads to defensive detachments: Better not to love than to love and lose. Individuals who fear relatedness because early love was soured by disappointment may continually seek attachments but, fearing disappointment, withdrawal from them or constantly vacillate between approach and avoidance.*[7]

We can't protect ourselves by detaching from life because we fear loss and disappointment—avoiding risk only deepens isolation and reinforces feelings of abandonment. The past does not have to dictate the future. Healing requires time, honesty, and the willingness to learn new emotional skills. By acknowledging where we are and understanding how the past shaped us, we create space for new outcomes. More importantly, growth comes through connection—with ourselves and with supportive people around us who encourage us to take chances, knowing that both wins and losses are part of living fully.

> Healing requires time, honesty, and the willingness to learn new emotional skills.

ENDNOTES

1. Schoenfelder, E.N., Sandler, I.N., Wolchik, S. *et al.* Quality of Social Relationships and the Development of Depression in Parentally-Bereaved Youth. *J Youth Adolescence* 40, 85–96 (2011). Retreived from https://doi.org/10.1007/s10964-009-9503-z on May 15, 2025.

2. Claudia. Jewett Jarratt. *Helping Children Cope with Separation and Loss.* (Boston: The Harvard Common Press.) 1994. 97

3. Ibid. 186.

4. Ibid. 15.

5. ibid. 12.

6. Ibid. 185.

7. Elizabeth. Waites. *Trauma and Survival. (New York: W.W, Norton and Company, Inc). 1994. 186.*

The Fear of Intimacy

*"The ability to trust others is
at the heart of intimacy."*

CLINTON AND SIBCY

always heard intimacy described as "in-to-me-see." It's a pretty good definition, actually, but for someone who was riddled with the fear of exposure, I wasn't going to let that happen! After all, I didn't want *anyone* to see in me. I was just beginning to see in me, and that was overwhelming, ugly, and grievous in and of itself.

In Don Carter's book, *Thawing Childhood Abandonment Issues,* he defines the term and states that *intimacy* is often viewed through the very narrow focus of sexual activity. This is a mistake. First of all, strangers can have sex and never be even remotely intimate in the true sense of the word. Secondly, healthy sexual intimacy is a reward for having built an authentically intimate relationship.[1]

I noticed a recurring pattern in my life. I was always overly eager to please. It seemed I always gave more in the relationship than others gave, only to be hurt and disappointed that the giving was not reciprocated. If people came on too strong, too fast, I could feel myself recoiling— okay, running in the opposite direction. Feeling that in all my relationships something was missing, but not being sure what that something was, which made me doubt myself—doubt myself *a lot.* I would put off making a decision; thus, a decision was made (not making a decision is a decision). I would go along fine for a while, then suddenly feel overwhelmed and discouraged. Maybe it was a project looming over my head or that I simply missed someone's birthday. Maybe it was an invitation to an event or just a "Hey, let's have coffee" that would steal my thunder and be the straw that broke the camel's back.

As a pastor, when a new person would visit the church and say, "We loved the service; we'll see you next Sunday," I would tell myself, "Well, that's probably the last time I will see them." Then, I would actually be surprised when they came back. That is no longer the case. At this stage in my journey, I expect them to return—they do, and we are growing at a rapid rate. But before we could do that, I had to grow first. Remember, we get what we expect.

For years, I would say I had the "Avoidant Attachment style." I would always disregard or ignore my own wants, needs, desires, and preferences to keep the peace. I would say to myself, "Who cares anyway?" "Don't rock the boat. After all, they might leave." I was determined to keep the peace at all costs. For me, conflict meant someone would leave me. I had thoughts of things like, "They probably won't even say goodbye." In the book *Attachments: Why You Love, Feel, and Act the Way You Do*, authors Dr. Tim Clinton and Dr. Gary Sibcy describe and provide insight into four specific attachment styles, principles, and dynamics. I am only providing you a brief glance into their extraordinary work on why you love, feel, and act the way you do. The following is a summary of their great work. I encourage you to purchase a copy of their book and explore further. Both authors emphasize that our strongest emotional expressions are tied to our closest relationships. Join me as we take a closer look at the author's perspective on the fear of intimacy and the four attachment styles.

The Avoidant Attachment Style:

Persons with the avoidant attachment style often struggle with at least one of these three areas of intimacy.

1. Avoidant Persons Struggle with the Emotional Connection

People with an avoidant attachment style find it difficult to listen sensitively to the thoughts and feelings of those they're closest to, their spouse or children. They see this sensitivity as a weakness. The avoidant person can be very desirous of relationships, even loving, yet those around this person may not know how much love (they are) giving or sharing. Instead, loved ones may feel very unloved and abandoned.

2. Avoidant Persons Struggle with Disclosure of Private Thoughts and Feelings

When you grow up feeling abandoned and rejected, you learn to hide those thoughts and experiences. You learn to distance yourself from your own feelings, even your own desire for emotional closeness.

By disclosing intimate thoughts and feelings, one becomes vulnerable to being hurt all over again. This vulnerability opens up one's thoughts and experiences to criticism and misinterpretation. And that is difficult and even scary to avoidant individuals.

3. Avoidant Persons Struggle with Nonsexual Touch

Interestingly, many avoidant people are turned off by tenderness and touch. That touchy-feely stuff can drive them crazy. Some counselors call this type of attachment "the protected self" because these people appear, and generally are, tough, and even hard, on the outside. Oh, they may be personable enough. Some are even the life of the party. But all this life and energy are used to keep people at a distance.

The closer you might get to avoidant people's hearts, the more threatened they may feel and the more defensive they may become.

The Avoidant Attachment Style has two relationship rules:

1. *The avoidant attachment style assumes other people are not reliable, dependable, or trustworthy when it comes to my needs.*

2. *They assume, "I must rely on myself alone in order to meet my needs." Others always let you down just when you need them the most.*

The Ambivalent Attachment Style

Those with the ambivalent attachment style are identified as a fragile self that develop filled with strong but ambivalent emotions. There is a tentativeness in their minds. Sometimes they feel intense love, sometimes intense hate. Their self-talk includes, "I am not worthy of love." "I am not capable of getting the love I need without being angry and clingy." "Others are capable of meeting my needs but might not do so because of my flaws." "Others are trustworthy and reliable but might abandon me because of my worthlessness." At the core of the Ambivalent Attachment Style is the concept of the fear of abandonment.

The Disorganized Attachment Style

Persons with a disorganized attachment style have the ability to find darkness everywhere they turn. As they look out at the world of relationships, the grass is always dead on both sides of the fence. They hold a negative view of others and a negative view of themselves. The result is a behavior that includes a mixed bag of attachment problems. They are often described as having a "shattered self."

"I am not worthy of love." "Others are unable to meet my needs."

"Others are not trustworthy or reliable."

The Secure Attachment Style

When secure people run into problems, they can experience the whole spectrum of emotions from joy to depression, from confusion to peace, and even anxiety, sadness, guilt, and, yes, anger. They experience the same emotions as the other attachment styles, with some definite characteristics that set them apart from the other attachment styles.

Secure attachments don't feel pressure to perform. They have confidence in who they are. They have an internal sense of security that frees them from all hidden and internal agendas that are present in other attachment styles.

They're not worried that they'll be harmed or emotionally bruised if others disapprove. Finally, they practice restraint like any loving and thoughtful person would. "I am worthy of love." "I am capable of getting the love and support I need." "Others are willing and able to love me." [2]

Did you see yourself in any of those styles? Take a moment to pause and consider what you just learned about yourself and how it impacts your relationships. If, like me, you choose to allow that self-awareness to guide growth, then keep reading. There is light at the end of this tunnel.

CHILDHOOD EMOTIONAL NEGLECT

Because of the Childhood Emotional Neglect (CEN), I would hear, "Shut up." Growing up, I was told, "Quit crying, or I'll give you something to cry about!" If I did speak my peace, it had been pent up for so long that it came out with true "West Virginia Style Sass." My mother was quick to back-hand me right in the mouth. I had many a bloody lip until I learned to duck. I am a fairly good "ducker." Even today, though there's never been a need to physically duck in a conversation with someone, I still respond emotionally with an invisible duck.

I never knew the tenderness of a mother until I was grown, and I went to visit her alone for a work trip. I spent the night at her home. For some reason, she came into my room and tucked me in. I was shocked. I was speechless. I couldn't find words. I just remember how wonderful that moment felt. I talk about this in the first book I wrote, *The ABC's of Being a Mother.* Having been abandoned at such a young age, I had a fear of not being a good mother. God consoled me one time on the matter and literally gave me the title and contents of that book.[3]

Let me share with you a sad story. My mother and I graduated from the same high school. I wanted to wear her high school ring so badly. After years of asking, she finally allowed me to wear it to school, and I lost it. I felt terrible. I knew the feeling of losing something that you had attached emotion to. I've searched for years for a replacement, a real

1955 UHS Class Ring (University High School). I still have not been able to find one. My mother was only eighteen when she delivered me, having gotten married in her senior year of high school. In one respect, I knew I need not fear the dreaded loss of the ring from my mother, but, on the other hand, I knew how much that ring meant to her, and still probably does today. So, I think that is one more reason why my life seemed so confusing. There were more good memories than bad ones, but there just were not a lot of memories.

In a blog article entitled "4 Types of Intimacy in Marriage Beyond Physical," I read about how couples need to cultivate these four types of intimacy in their relationship:

> *One,* **emotional intimacy** *allows you to connect more deeply with your spouse through sharing thoughts and feelings. It involves telling each other your deepest fears, dreams, disappointments, complicated emotions, and feeling seen and understood when you do.*

> *Two is* **intellectual intimacy.** *Emotional intimacy leads to intellectual intimacy. When neither of you worries about potential conflicts when sharing thoughts and feelings, each person feels the freedom to have valued individual opinions.*

> *Three is* **experiential intimacy,** *and it's when people bond during leisure activities. It's about*

sharing your day-to-day experience and getting closer together. Each person in the relationship has particular roles and interests. The key is to make sure that some of those things overlap so you are doing things together.

*Four is **spiritual intimacy,** and it's more than spending time in God's word. It's learning how to connect with each other through your faith.*

Of the four intimacy types, I find intellectual intimacy and spiritual intimacy the most facile to engage in. I struggle with emotional intimacy and experiential intimacy. They come as more of a challenge. I believe the reason being is if I feel stress or anxiety in the moment, I will tend to dissociate.

Louis Breger defines dissociation as:

"The ability to psychologically cleave off thoughts, feelings, and even physical pain, and shift the experience to some other part of the consciousness. Young children are prone to use dissociation as a way to cope with life's normal anxieties. The essence of dissociation ... is to be found in the typical ways in which a child meets a conflict he cannot resolve in reality; that is by splitting himself off from such reality and 'solving' conflicts in play or fantasy ... Fantasy solutions to

conflict involve an abandonment of a direct or 'real' solution for a "pretend" or imaginary one.[4]

I'm not sure where I go when I dissociate, but I do make an intentional effort to stay present now. I was not capable or even aware that I did this in the past. I have huge time lapses in my memory. I just can't remember the details of events sometimes. I will remember that I went somewhere, but because of the stress and anxiety, I forgot who was there or what we did while we were there. In the *Body Keeps the Score,* Dr. Bessel van der Kolk explains the science of repressed memory:

Memory loss has been reported in people who have experienced natural disasters, accidents, war trauma, kidnapping, torture, concentration camps, and physical and sexual abuse. Total memory loss is most common in childhood sexual abuse, with incidence ranging from 19 percent to 38 percent.[5]

Dr. van der Kolk goes on to explain that as early as 1980, the *Diagnostic Manual of Mental Disorders* (DSM-III) recognized the existence of memory loss for traumatic events in the diagnostic criteria for dissociative amnesia, defined as:

An inability to recall important personal information, usually of a traumatic or stressful nature, that is too extensive to be explained by normal forgetfulness. Memory loss has been part

of the criteria for PTSD since that diagnosis was
first introduced.[6]

It's not enough for someone to say they love me; they have to *show* me. One way of showing me is simply staying. When you think about that, it's pretty sad. You can treat me badly or totally ignore me, not meet any of my emotional needs, but just be there, and I think that's love. At least, that is the way it was. Not anymore. I now require empathy and respect. I'm a recovering co-dependent due to the abandonment I experienced. Knowing this makes it easier for me to accept as well as expect to be treated lovingly and with respect. Remember, we teach and train people how to treat us.

If you are critical or preoccupied, angry, or dismissive toward me, I find it much easier to go where I am celebrated rather than stay where I am tolerated. I can take being misunderstood if you are trying to relate, but if I sense you are trying to control me, I'm out. This is a huge triumph for me. Healing is freeing.

My parents both suffered from Childhood Emotional Neglect (CEN). They worked hard. They took care of themselves. They were and are tough and resilient. I got that from them. However, because of that, they expected my siblings and me to take on age-inappropriate responsibilities. I was carrying a baby on my hip from as far back as I can remember, and I don't even have hips. As an adult, I avoided closeness and was far more attracted to others who avoided intimacy as well. If you wanted a superficial relationship that is all work and no play, I was all in.[7]

"T.M.I."

Another issue I must keep in check is "T.M.I."—too much information—a fear of revealing too much about myself and then panicking because I really don't trust others not to share my information. I fear that by sharing too much, I will drive others away. I battled such low self-esteem that I always thought people knew so much more than me. So why should I share what I knew? But hey, you get it. That's why you picked up this book. But you know what? Your journey has taught you much. There is an audience waiting for you who wants to hear your story too. You may not write a book, but you may teach a class, raise children, break generational curses in your family bloodline, or even be a CEO who can manage people no one else could because you get it.

Repeatedly, I learned the hard way that if you rely on someone to take care of you, they will probably let you down. So, I engrained in my mind, "Take care of yourself," "Take care of yourself ..." hence, the *Blue Jean Jacket*. I often found myself more concerned about my personal inanimate belongings than people, which left me to be much of a loner in my heart, though it looked to others quite the opposite. Such was the case in college.

I lived with four other girls but took the attic room where I could live with my plants and my cat. I felt forced to fend for myself for as long as I can remember. Eat hotdogs and coleslaw because that's all I could afford. I had this inner drive to defend myself. I had to give people reasons for why I did what I did. I occasionally slip up on this, even today. They could have cared less, and later in life, I was always accused of "T.M.I." too much information, which just reinforced that I was alone, I should shut up, and stay that way. I didn't believe anyone really cared.

It turns out that I was right and wrong: right about no one caring about all the details. Right in that, I didn't have to give an excuse or a reason for everything I did or every decision I made. I was a grown adult. I wanted to join in with my roommates, but we really had nothing in common. They all went home for the summer, and I got free rent for keeping up with all the utility bills and upkeep on the house. I was a workaholic, earning my keep. In *Healing the Shame that Binds You*, John Bradshaw describes it like this:

> *The drivenness in any addiction is about the ruptured self, the belief one is flawed as a person. The content of the addiction, whether it be an ingestive addiction or an activity addiction (such as work, shopping, or gambling), is an attempt at an intimate relationship. The workaholic with his work and the alcoholic with his booze are having a love affair. Each one alters the mood to avoid the feeling of loneliness and hurt in the underbelly of shame. Each addictive acting out creates life-damaging consequences that create more shame. The new shame fuels the cycle of the addiction.*[8]

My roommates came back in the fall with all their belongings just the way they left them. I just treated them like they were my kids too. Now, I realize I didn't know how to be a college student and one of them. I grew up to be a dysfunctional adult at thirteen. So, even if they knew something I didn't, if they were more stable and better functioning than me, I could not have been convinced. I was a controlling know-it-all! Everything had to be done my way. After all, I knew it all. Life experiences told me I was the boss.

Coming to terms with the truth that I was underdeveloped in my emotional intelligence was an extremely humbling revelation.

Coming to terms with the truth that I was underdeveloped in my emotional intelligence was an extremely humbling revelation. However, the good side is that I am so teachable. I will be the first to admit I do not know everything. I am now totally guard down and ready to learn what I don't know.

CORE BELIEFS

We all have core beliefs. Mine were mostly ungodly, dysfunctional, and self-sabotaging in all relationships. When faced with a problem I would always jump to the worst-case scenario. "They're dead!" "Someone stole it!" "They hate me!" "We're all gonna die!" "I'm gonna die!" This left people thinking I was too much drama to deal with. In reality, I *was* a lot of drama. I always said to those closest to me, "I get on my own nerves!" And I did.

Once, I almost drowned. I slipped on the green, slimy, mossy rock of a babbling creek along my favorite biking trail. I lost my balance and was headed over the turbulent falls while arguing with the one person who was there who could save my life. She had to escalate to get me to hear her—literally, scream my name and directions so she could help me. She had to shout louder than the voice in my head to get me just to trust her to take her hand, to keep me from dropping to my death.

Abandoned people can be so stubborn.

> **Without healing, we will abandon ourselves and, thus, suffer in the area of intimacy.**

Are you nodding in agreement? Trust is hard for those of us who were abandoned. We need to be healed. I needed to be healed. Without healing, we will abandon ourselves and, thus, suffer in the area of intimacy.

For some reason, once I am in the trauma cycle, the voice of the person speaking must be loud enough to drown out my own inner voice, or I can't hear them. Then, I get my feelings hurt because they yelled at me. Yeah, it still happens, but not nearly as often. I know this behavior and the lack of trust originate from trauma and are my mode of operation. I give myself a little more kindness and do a lot of healthy self-talk to bring myself back to reality.

You see, I had always struggled with this deeply held belief that I was the flawed acorn. The flawed acorn grew into an oak that nothing and no one could shake free of the fear of intimacy. Until one day, I refused to stay an acorn hidden in the recesses of my soul. I realize now my actions were self-protective measures to elude closeness, intimacy, trust, and dependency. The pain of rejection would have been more than I could have handled. I was, at one point in my life, too fragile to even be corrected. I took correction as rejection and directives as control and manipulation.

I am grateful that the God who created me loved me enough to put people in my life who constantly confronted me with love and acceptance—even when I could not recognize it as such. I am grateful I took a class that smacked me in the face and made me realize the root of my issues. I am grateful for the desire to be healed, healthy, and whole and the wiring to seek out answers and apply wisdom to my life. I decided to trust that the abandoned little girl inside me could be set free and finally pass into an accepted, adored, confident adult.

And that decision changed everything.

Our core beliefs cause us to make decisions based on lies rather than truth. The truth is that some people do love you.

The truth is that some people do have your best interest at heart. I remember an acquaintance; we will call her Kathleen, who believed the lie that her father told her about not being pretty enough, not skinny enough, and that she would never find a man or have children. She went as far as allowing a man to move in with her and take her for all she was worth. She believed her father. She expected what her father said to come to pass. Broke and homeless, she reached out for help.

She got the help she needed, and today, she is successful, beautiful, and financially well-off.

If you have been abandoned and can find just one person to believe in you, who will applaud your accomplishments, disregard your failures, and allow you to process—hold on to them. They are the true treasures in life.

Even if you once feared intimacy, recognize it as a sacred invitation to turn inward and connect with the child you once were—the one who was left waiting, wondering, and aching to be seen. The echoes of abandonment and neglect may have taught you how to perform and prove yourself in the hopes of being chosen. But healing begins when you lay down those burdens and listen to the quiet truth beneath the noise: *you were always worthy.*

As you gently untangle the false beliefs that have shaped your story, you make room for something truer and more whole. Embracing healthy connections with people who provide you with the safety of being known without performance, and the abandoned child within you will find rest. There, in the slow unfolding of trust, you can rediscover intimacy not as a danger but as a gift.

It is a place where you are no longer too much or not enough but simply, beautifully, *you*.

Healing begins when you lay down your burdens and listen to the quiet truth beneath the noise: *you were always worthy.*

ENDNOTES

1. Don, Carter, MSW, LCSW. *Thawing Childhood Abandonment Issues.* Don Carter, MSW, LCSW, 2016. P. 164.

2. Tim, Clinton, and Gary, Sibcy. *Attachments, Why You Love Feel and Act the Way You Do.* (Brentwood: Integrity Publishers). 2002. pages 49-56, 75-79, 95-96, 125-128.

3. You can visit my website www.RenaPerozich. com to order The ABC's of Being a Mother.

4. Eagle Family Ministries blog entitled "4 Types of Intimacy in Marriage Beyond Physical." By Eagle Family Admin March 30, 2022 https://www.eaglefamily.org/4-types-of-intimacy-in-marriage-beyond-physical.

5. E.F. Loftus, S. Polonsky, and M. T. Fullilove, "Memories of Childhood Sexual Abuse: Remembering and Repressing," Psychology of Women Quarterly 18, no. 1 (1994): 67-84. L.M. Williams, "Recall of Childhood Trauma: A prospective Study of Women's memories of Child Sexual Abuse," *Journal of Consulting and Clinical Psychology,* 62, no.6 (1994): 1167-76.

6. Bessel. van der Kolk. *The Body Keeps The Score.* (New York: Penguin Books). 2014. p. 192

7. A great resource on understanding codependency is written by Darlene Lancer, JD, LMFT entitled *Codependency: 8 Steps to seeing the True You.* You can find more information about her at www.whatiscodependency.com and even get a free copy of "14 Tips for Letting Go."

8. John, Bradshaw. *Healing The Shame That Binds You.* (Deerfield Beach: Health Communications, Inc.) 2005. P. 35-36.

Dissociation

"One day, you will tell your story of how you overcame what you went through, and it will be someone else's survival guide."

BRENE BROWN

This is, without a doubt, the most difficult and frightening chapter I've ever written. It's also the one that has sparked the most conflict in my life—fights with my spouse, my children, siblings, and friends. For years, I believed something was fundamentally wrong with me. Eventually, I was diagnosed with ADHD, along with anxiety, depression (though I still question that one), and the ever-present shadow of abandonment. These things together formed a picture of Complex PTSD (CPTSD). One of the most distressing symptoms for me was my memory: large gaps where significant events or serious conversations should have been. I couldn't recall details, and that invariably frustrated *everyone* around me. (Yes, I still fall into using words like "always," "never," and "everyone"—a habit common among those who've felt abandoned.) But it wasn't just forgetfulness. It wasn't lack of attention, nor was it Alzheimer's or dementia—both of which I was tested for and definitively ruled out. I wasn't using drugs, despite my kids jokingly suggesting otherwise. And no, it wasn't a traumatic blow to the head—at least not in the traditional sense. The trauma was deeper. It was abandonment in my childhood. That was the wound that shaped it all.

When I was learning to walk, my father always told the story of how I fell up the concrete steps and hit my head right between and above my eyes and nose. He continued the story of how it swelled up and how black both my eyes got. He said he worried that I might have really hurt myself, and how he held me. Interestingly, there was never a word about taking me to the doctor to get a check-up. Every memory my pen finds to share with you on paper, my mind is confronted with more Childhood Emotional Neglect (CEN), trauma, and ADHD symptoms.

I remember very little about my childhood. My brothers also have very few memories of their childhood. There have been rumors of violations and abuses not mentioned within these pages due to being left alone, left with several varying caregivers and people we didn't even know. We were allowed to go to anyone's house and spend the night wherever and with whomever. Our parents were always working, never around. Although my parents were never intentionally hurtful or vengeful, they were neglectful. In hindsight, I can see how they loved us the best way they knew how. They carried their own unresolved struggles—struggles that had no name and of which they had no awareness. Those unspoken wounds became patterns, and those patterns became the cycle we inherited.

Those unspoken wounds became patterns, and those patterns became the cycle we inherited.

As I became an adult, I could sense my brain shutting down because my pain was so great. I was incapable of coping with my fears. These fears varied from normal childhood uncertainties to dramatic scenarios that I would imagine. Even as an adult, the dreaded "What Ifs?" would start, and then I would loop again or dissociate. I would just be gone. I would stare off into nothingness at times, and people would ask, "Are you listening?" I was, but I wasn't. I couldn't explain. I could hear them audibly, but I had stopped consciously processing what they were saying. At other times, the performer in me would take over, and no one would notice. My body, my eye contact, head nods, and maybe even a vocal "uh-huh" would be there—but I wasn't.

I would push myself past any physical limits, trying to do my part, carry my load, and share the burden. This pattern became dangerously apparent on a long car trip with a friend. The grown-up child who had experienced abandonment by others refused to abandon anyone else. Exhausted, I continued my share of the driving. My friend was riding shotgun, trying to get some sleep so she could relieve me in a little bit and we could continue the journey.

A few times, I hit the rumble strip and was jarred, as was my sleeping friend. "You okay?" she said. "Yeah! I'm good." I continued a conversation with her while swerving all over the road. I hit the rumble strip a few more times, and my friend screamed at me and woke me up. My dissociation, apparently, was able to perform while awake or asleep. She said that I carried on a complete conversation with her all the while I was sleeping. I mean, I have heard of sleepwalking, but sleep-driving?

Many times in my marriage, my husband would say he had a conversation with me the night before, and I wouldn't even remember. Friends would say, "I was just talking away, and you were engaging with me, and then I realized you were gone." For the most part, I lived exhausted. I just wanted to get away. Just sleep.

My life has been marked by countless episodes of dissociation, but instead of revisiting each one, I would like to focus on how I'm learning to cope and move forward.

1. **When I am tired, I say so.** I don't pretend I am full of energy and try to go along with the crowd or push myself to please others.

2. **I set limits and boundaries for myself.** This is a hard thing I had to learn to do as an adult. Usually, our parents teach us this skill as a child by either modeling, mirroring, or instruction.

3. **I will tell people to write it down and email me.** Send me a Slack message, instant message me— whatever they want to do so I don't have to rely on my memory. We train people how to treat us.

4. **When in a crowd or in uncomfortable situations, I consciously make myself stay present.** I will use my five senses to ground myself. (a) Where am I? (b) Who is with me? (c) Why am I here? (d) What do I want to remember about this moment or event? (e) Then, I consciously file it in my memory so I can retrieve it later.

This last one has always been particularly helpful to me. Before, people would say, "Remember when we went to _____, and you and I _____?" (You can fill in the blanks.) They could tell by my face that I hadn't a clue what they were talking about. Because the situation was either so stressful or I was so overwhelmed, I simply and robotically went through the motions, robbing me of not just the experience but the memories.

I mastered the art of deflecting, just like a boxer in the ring. I dodged conversations, compliments, corrections, instructions, touchy subjects, and life blows from my opponent in the ring. If I didn't want to discuss a matter or the subject hit too close to home or triggered pain, I deflected and went back to my corner. However, unlike the professional boxer, I had no coach to slap my face and bring me back to the present, douse me with a bucket of water (truth), and encourage me to stay present, use the tools I have acquired, and stay in the ring.

Our past is always willing to take us back. I dealt with dissociation in many ways. I had an unhealthy separation anxiety—an extreme fear that bad things would happen to important people in my life if I were not with them. Any time I feel emotional distance, either present in a room I walk into or a relationship I have, or if there is silence in a conversation where no one says a word, these things trigger me. I feel that something is wrong, and if something is wrong, someone is going to leave. I fear I will be abandoned again.

So, since I have trouble regulating my moods, trusting people, and dealing with anxiety, at times, I dissociate from people altogether. If I have no feelings for a person, if they go away, abandon, or neglect me, I will be okay. Dissociation, to me, is a preoccupation with being okay. I have this inner drive to just be okay. I don't want to hurt. I don't want to be rejected. I don't want you to die or go away. Can we just be friends? Can we just love one another—forever?

Reality responds to these questions with a loud, resounding "No" that drowns out all the gentle, well-meaning, kind, and sincere "Yeses" offered by others. When your thoughts are distorted, your emotions follow suit—and when your emotions deceive you, your actions begin to lose their grounding in truth.

I had no vocabulary to address, assign meaning, or help me through this process, but through my studies, I have learned that I suffer from what psychiatrists call *"Alexithymia,"* a word describing difficulty in identifying, describing, and experiencing my emotions. In essence, a "lack of words" and "emotional blindness." Many traumatized children and adults simply cannot describe what they are feeling because they cannot identify what their physical sensations mean. They may look furious but deny that they are angry; they may appear terrified but say that they are fine.

Not being able to discern what is going on inside your body causes you to be out of touch with your needs, and you have trouble taking care of yourself. Things as simple as eating the right amount of food at appropriate times and getting enough sleep are a challenge.

In her book *Black Swan,* Susan Anderson writes:

> *Abandonment is a complex human issue; its wound deeply entrenched in fear and insecurity. Without recovery, abandonment can linger beneath the surface, undermining self-esteem and sabotaging future relationships.[1]*

UNHEALED WOUNDS
BECOME INHERITED PAIN

There's another form of dissociation I rarely hear discussed—one that happens between us and our own children. It's the kind that arises when we believe, often unconsciously, that we lack the emotional intelligence (EQ) to face confrontation. On the surface, we may not realize it, but the abandoned child within us knows all too well. Instead of addressing difficult issues, we avoid them. We stay silent, pretend it never happened, and, as the saying goes, "sweep it under the rug." But eventually, we trip over it. And by the time we do, the room may already reek from all we've buried there. It's far better to face things honestly and in the moment than to let emotional debris pile up until it overwhelms us and those we love.

In *Adult Children of Emotionally Immature Parents,* Lindsay Gibson observes:

> *Emotional immaturity is a real phenomenon that has been studied and written about for a long time. It undermines people's ability to deal with stress and to be emotionally intimate with others. Emotionally immature people often grew up in a family environment that curtailed their full emotional and intellectual development. As a result, they have an over simplified approach to life, narrowing situations down to fit their rigid*

coping skills. Having such a limited sense of self makes them egocentric and undermines their ability to be sensitive to other people's needs and feelings. They have reactive emotions and a lack of objectivity, especially when it comes to their children.[2]

I wanted to be present for my children. I was physically there, but I was not always emotionally there. They were always clean, well-fed, well-dressed, engaged in outside activities, had many friends, and invited their friends to our home to swim in our pool. I kept the house, the garden, the laundry up, and meals made. I thought I was doing it all right. Looking back, many days, I was going through the motions, trying not to fall apart. I was trying to live the life I did not have a chance to live when I was a child, *and* be a perfect parent in all areas of my life at the same time.

As a child, no one told me that I had to choose between basketball or band. So, I just did both. I would fill every minute of every day for myself and my children. Otherwise, I felt like either my children or I would miss out on something. Enough was never enough. My fragile nervous system would have to dissociate to find peace and rest because, emotionally, I was never taught how to regulate. The teapot was always on high heat, and the steam was constantly being released in no particular direction. I was just going through the motions as fast as I could. My children lived in a rush. Hurry here. Hurry, get ready. Hurry, let's leave. I have laundry to do. You have baths to take. I was still running the house like I did as an adolescent and teenager. There was a dissociation between me and real life.

Looking back, I carry deep regrets over the way my unhealed wounds shaped my parenting. Before I understood what was truly going on inside me—before I had language for abandonment, dissociation, or the drive to fix what felt broken—I moved through motherhood in a constant state of hyper-urgency. I pushed, rushed, and hurried my children through life, not realizing that my own unmet needs were setting the pace.

I wish I could go back and be more present, more gentle, and more attuned. But I can't. My children are grown now, raising little ones of their own. What I *can* do is show up *now*—with honesty, humility, and a willingness to repair. I can apologize, listen deeply, and help them make sense of what they may have carried from me. Together, we can break this generational cycle so that my grandchildren can grow up rooted in secure, loving, and fully present relationships.

> What I *can* do is show up *now*— with honesty, humility, and a willingness to repair.

But it has to start with me. I'm learning—slowly, patiently, and with grace—to stay present even when it's uncomfortable. To not rush. To trust God's timing. And above all, to remember—because presence, not perfection, is what begins the healing.

In the appendix, you'll find a carefully curated bibliography and resource list—tools to support you on your path from abandonment to acceptance. This isn't just information; it's part of the legacy I long to leave behind. My deepest hope, my earnest prayer, is that you, I, and every reader who finds these words will live out our days in true freedom. Freedom from the enemies that harm the body, torment the soul, and silence the spirit. May we rise above our abandonment—identify the triggers so we can respond and not react, confront our fears and find courage, trade shame for truth and compassion, and bring into the light every shadow that tries to steal our peace and convince us that we are anything less than whole, worthy, and deeply loved.

ENDNOTES

1. Susan, Anderson. *Black Swan*. (Huntington, NY. Rock Foundation Press). 1999, viii.
2. Lindsay, Gibson. *Adult Children of Emotionally Immature Parents*. (Oakland, CA. New Harbinger Publications, Inc.) 2015, 47.

C H A P T E R   T W E L V E

Wearing A New Jacket

"Never Give Up!
WINSTON CHURCHILL

Today, I have a great relationship with my mother. This in itself is a miracle, and I wish to acknowledge it with gratitude. My mother repented of her sins, received the gift of salvation, and is going to Heaven. I cannot tell you what joy that brings me.

Another miracle I received that many children of emotional abandonment will never get is that my mother apologized to me. Honestly, this brought on a storm of conflicting emotions—relief, sorrow, anger, hope, joy—all tangled together. For years, I carried the weight of being left behind, and now, in a few words, she acknowledged the pain and asked for my forgiveness.

It's what every child dreams of.

And when an apology comes, we are challenged to accept the apology and release them from the burden of having to pay us back somehow or make it up to us. Can we forgive? Can we let it go? We know we need to in order to move on. But can we?

Her apology didn't erase the past, but it made my pain feel real—not just to me, but to her. The acknowledgment was validation I never expected to receive. Again, I am grateful.

But an apology isn't a time machine. It doesn't give back holidays, birthdays, or the childhood and adolescence I navigated without her. But it is a moment of truth, and that has healing significance. I was on the path to healing regardless because healing is not dependent on closure. But her apology reminded me not so much of what I had lost but how strong I had become in the process of the journey.

Long after I threw in the towel, my husband of 48 years refused to give up on my mother and her complete deliverance and reconciliation. In truth, he suffered from the abandonment I experienced almost as much as I did. He lived with a hurricane—a tempest in a teacup, spilling emotional instability, control, and anxiety at random intervals, but he kept me safe. He was always the eye of the storm. My lack of trust, intimacy, health, wealth, and ability to function in a happy, thriving relationship would have been much harder without someone who just refused to leave. I may have worried others might go, but deep down, I always knew he was there for good.

Relationships function as emotional systems, and when one member changes—for good or bad—it forces everyone else to adjust because the old formula no longer works. If one person rewrites their script and begins to heal, set boundaries, and behave differently, it changes the narrative for everyone they are in relationship with. Every person connected has no choice but to respond and adapt to the new story.

I changed little by little each day. As I changed, all my relationships changed. Some may not have liked the no-longer-a-performing-perfectionist, dysfunctional me, but I can't name one. However, the pages in this book could not contain the number of people that I have helped, resourced, mentored, taught, or coached to become a better version of themselves. When you become the healed and whole version you were created to be, then *and only then* can you fulfill your God-given purpose—to live as the person you were created and designed to be.

I finished writing this book around my firstborn's forty-fifth birthday. It was the greatest birthday gift I could give her, for in so doing, her mother's legacy will live long. This book will bring healing and deliverance and perhaps an epiphany to others—maybe even you ...

Adulthood gives us the privilege to change our story, one chapter at a time. The pages you have read may have awakened hurts, triggered thoughts, feelings, and actions. Perhaps reading my story brought you to tears or made you want to want to quit. Don't. Read it through again. Mark up the pages. Underline, highlight, tab, and buy one for someone you love. Journal through your feelings—write it, read it, rehearse it. Be resilient. Embrace what happened and take it all, wrap it up, and give it to the world as a gift.

You already survived all the pain and trauma, so now it doesn't have to hurt anyone anymore. Honesty about what happened isn't a betrayal; facing it is courageous, and denial will keep you locked in the cell of your past. Remember, you are not what happened to you or what you even did to others in your woundedness.

> **Honesty about what happened isn't betrayal; facing it is courageous, and denial will keep you locked in the cell of your past.**

I carefully curated a list of resources for you at the end of this book—a bibliotherapy to help guide you on your healing journey. I have learned vulnerability can build community. I truly did not find my people until I shared my story. For me, it all began when I got a coach. His name was

Dr. Keith Johnson. It was sitting in the middle of one of his classes that my first rude awakening—the epiphany that led to my healing journey—occurred.[1]

I highly suggest you find a coach who will mentor you and call out the good things in you. Find a coach who will tell you the truth, even when that truth is painful. Why? Because they care enough about you to see beyond the present pain and push you to the power of your potential. It is *never* too late to rewire your brain. I am in the last year of my sixties, and I am still rewiring, and I love my life.

You cannot change people. And you don't need to. Changing you is enough.

I consider every author I read as a coach, and through this book, I can coach you, too. I invite you to use this book, the companion journal, the resources in the bibliotherapy, and all the tools you have learned along this journey to guide your progress. I'll even go a step further and invite you to coach with me personally—one on one. I will see you. Hear you. Value what is inside of you, and do all in my power to point you in the direction of healing. Visit my website to learn more about that.

You can learn more and take your own #Branded Abandoned Assessment. I would love to hear your story. I want to help you through your journey and equip you to do the same for others! Someone is waiting for what you have to offer. So, here is your invitation to the Big Table. Go to:

WWW.RENAPEROZICH.COM

Because until you have allowed yourself to acknowledge what happened to you and grieve what was missing from your life, it is hard to move forward. Until you are healed, you will be stuck in the cycle of disappointment, fear, loss, anxiety … and all that goes with those things.

Few of us understand what forgiveness truly is, and that misconception keeps us from exercising one of the most powerful tools in our arsenal for mental health. Forgiveness doesn't mean excusing harmful behavior. It isn't about letting someone off the hook; it's about freeing yourself from the grip of resentment and pain. You can forgive someone AND hold boundaries. You can release the anger without reopening the door to more hurt. You can forgive even if you never get an apology.

Forgiveness isn't about closure—it's about freedom. And growth. And healing. And empowerment. It's about releasing the weight of the past—not erasing it. It's a way to walk forward without dragging the chain of pain behind you.

For most of us, forgiveness is not a single event. It unfolds slowly over time, little by little. Advance and retreat. Heal and pick open the scab and heal again. But as the deeper work of healing and recovery progresses, the sharp edges of anger will start to soften. The more forgiveness you embrace, the more open space you create in your life for wholeness. Every tear you shed that releases sorrow or anger makes more room in your heart for compassion to flourish.

Your body and your emotions are hopelessly entwined. One can't be whole while the other is sick. A shift in one ripples through to the other. Decide today that you want to be healed. Decide that living free is more important than holding on to the right to be a victim. Once you have made the decision to heal, forgiveness will follow.

At its own pace. But it will follow.

WEARING MY NEW JACKET

So today, I can still wear my black dress and strappy black sandles with my faithful Ole' Blue—my blue jean jacket, but I wear it with a new confidence and a renewed assurance that I am okay. *I am going to be okay.* **You are going to be okay.** We may be different, but that is part of our secret sauce.

So be saucy!

I am right there with you.

Everywhere I go, everyone who sees me notices something is different about me, and they just can't put their finger on it. More importantly, I am different. I love the new blue jean jacket that I wear on the inside—the one no one sees, but I know that the change in me shows. It is okay for me to visit the past, but I do not want to live there—the future is way too wonderful.

On the day my mom walked out, we never said goodbye to each other. The hardest goodbyes are the ones we never got to say. Truthfully, it took me until this last chapter to realize why certain things, little things, are such big things to me. The end of this book isn't me walking away from you; it is honoring what we both need. So, I leave you with this—

You are not forgotten. You are not forsaken. You are held in love.

"I love you—bye."

ENDNOTE

1. For more on Dr. Keith Johnson, America's #1 Confidence Coach, visit www.drkeithjohnson.com. Tell him I sent you.

ABOUT THE AUTHOR

Dr. Rena Perozich is a passionate pastor, author, and international speaker whose prophetic ministry and healing anointing have impacted lives across more than 20 nations. A native of West Virginia, she is the founder and host of Women of Witness, a multi-denominational ministry that empowers women to discover their God-given purpose and build Christ-centered relationships.

She serves as Senior Elder at Restoration Church International and is ordained through MFC Ministries. With decades of experience as a teacher, mentor, pastoral counselor, and deliverance minister, Dr. Rena is widely respected for her prophetic insight, spiritual wisdom, and deep compassion for people.

Her published works include *The ABCs of Being a Mother, Moments That Matter, Fight Don't Fear,* and *The Blue Jean Jacket,* which is accompanied by a reflective journal. All are available on Amazon.

Dr. Rena maintains an active online presence, offering biblical encouragement and teaching through social media, and co-hosts *Believe Right,* a weekly television broadcast aired both regionally and online with her husband, Joe. She also hosts *The Answer to Your Prayers,* a shortwave radio program reaching 3.7 billion listeners in multiple languages via Hope Radio. In addition, she is a regular contributor to the bi-monthly column *Love & Marriage.*

Learn more at

RENAPEROZICH.COM

B I B L I O T H E R A P Y

Anderson, S. (1999). *Black Swan: The Twelve Lessons of Abandonment Recovery* (Illustrated ed.). Rock Foundations Press.

Anderson, S. (2016). *Abandonment Recovery Workbook: Guided meditation to Breaking the Chains of Rejection and Abandonment and Achieve Healing for hurts, Hardships, and Fears*. Caroline Pensabene.

Barkley, R. (2010). *Taking Charge of Adult ADHD*. The Guilford Press.

Black, C. (1999). *Changing Course-Healing from Loss, Abandonment, and Fear, Second Edition*. Hazelden Publishing.

Bradshaw, J. (1996). *Family Secrets - The Path from Shame to Healing*. Bantam.

Bradshaw, J. (2005). *Healing The Shame That Binds You*. Health Communications, Inc.

Bradshaw, J. (2009). *Reclaiming Virtue*. Bantam.

Campos, L. (2010). *Introduce Your Relationship To Transactional Analysis: A TA Primer, Third Edition.*

Carter, D. (2012). *Thawing Childhood Abandonment Issues (Thawing the Iceberg Series).* CreateSpace Independent Publishing Platform.

Clinton, T., & Sibcy, G. (2002). *Attachments: Why You Love, Feel, and Act the Way You Do.* Integrity Publishers.

Cloud, H. (2018). *Changes That Heal: Four Practical Steps to a Happier, Healthier You.* Zondervan.

Cori, J. (2017). *The Emotionally Absent Mother: How to Recognize and Heal the Invisible Effects of Childhood Emotional Neglect, Second Edition.* The Experiment, LLC.

Covey, S. M., Covey, S. R., & Merrill, R. R. (2018). *The SPEED of Trust: The One Thing That Changes Everything* (Reprint ed.). FREE PRESS.

Dobson, J. (1980). *Emotions Can You Trust Them.* World Wide Publications.

Ellis, A. & Harper, R. (1997). *A Guide to Rational Living. Third Edition.* Melvin Powers Wilshire Book Company.

Gibson, L. (2015). *Adult Children of Emotionally Immature Parents: How to Heal from Distant, Rejecting, or Self-Involved Parents.* New Harbinger Publications, Inc.

Glasser, W. (1998). *Choice Therapy.* HarperCollins Publishers.

Glasser, W. (1975). *Reality Therapy: A New Approach to Psychiatry.* (Paperback Edition) Harper & Row Publishers.

Groeschel, C. (2021). *Winning the War in Your Mind: Change Your Thinking, Change Your Life*. Zondervan.

Hayes, N. (2015). *Divine Healing: God's Recipe for Life & Health* (Reprint ed.). Harrison House Publishers.

Herman, J. (1997). *Trauma and Recovery: The Aftermath of Violence-From Domestic Abuse to Political Terror*. Basic Books.

Islieb, M. A. (2000). *Healing Toxic Emotions*. Insight Pub Group.

Kylstra, C., Kylstra, B., & Hamon, B. (2014). *Biblical Healing and Deliverance: A Guide to Experiencing Freedom from Sins of the Past, Destructive Beliefs, Emotional and Spiritual Pain, Curses and Oppression* (Repackaged ed.). Chosen Books.

Leaf, C., Turner, R., & Amua-Quarshie, P. (2019). *Think, Learn, Succeed: Understanding and Using Your Mind to Thrive at School, the Workplace, and Life* (Illustrated ed.). Baker Books.

Levine, P. & Frederick, A. *Waking the Tiger: Healing Trauma*. (1997). North Atlantic Books.

McGraw, P. C. (1999). *Life Strategies: Doing What Works, Doing What Matters* (1st ed.). Hachette Books.

McManus, E. R. (2017). *The Last Arrow: Save Nothing for the Next Life* (Reprint ed.). WaterBrook.

Pelzer, D. (1995). *A Child Called It: One Child's Courage to Survive* (Reissue ed.). Health Communications Inc.

Pelzer, D. (1997). *The Lost Boy: A Foster Child's Search for the Love of a Family* (Rev. ed.). Health Communications.

Pelzer, D. (2004). *The Privilege of Youth: A Teenager's Story* (Reprint ed.). Plume.

Pelzer, D. J. (2000). *A Man Named Dave*. Plume.

Perry, B. D. (2017). *Boy Who Was Raised as a Dog* (3rd ed.). Basic Books.

Rohn, J., & Reynolds, R. L. (1981). *Seasons of Life* (17th ed.). Jim Rohn Intl.

Rosier, T. (2021). *Your Brain's Not Broken: Strategies for Navigating Your Emotions and Life with ADHD*. Revell.

Rothschild, B. (2000). *The Body Remembers: The Psychophysiology of Trauma and Trauma Treatment (Norton Professional Book)* (Illustrated ed.). W. W. Norton & Company.

Seamands, D. A. (1981). *Healing for Damaged Emotions*. Adfo Books.

Seamands, D. A. (2015). *Healing for Damaged Emotions*. David C Cook.

Slough, T., Walters, W. K., Day, J., Garner, B. S., & Slough, R. (2020). *Not Yet: Finding Freedom When Anxiety, Depression, and Other Crap Come Knocking at Your Door*. Cross Timbers Community Church.

Smalley, G. (2004). *The DNA of Relationships*. Alive Publications, Inc.

Smeltzer, K. M., Smeltzer, Z. D., & Sandford, J. L. (2017). *Who Do You Say I Am?: Overcoming the Spirit of Identity Theft*. Destiny Oak.

Sokol, L & Fox, M. (2009). *Think Confident, Be Confident: A Four -Step Program to Eliminate Doubt and Achieve Lifelong Self-Esteem. Penguin Books, Ltd.*

Terradez, C., & Duplantis, C. (2021). *Fearless: Breaking the Habit of Fear.* Harrison House Publishers.

van der Kolk, B. (2014). *The Body Keeps the Score & Workbook for The Body Keeps The Score by Bessel van der Kolk M.D Paperback – JAN 2022.* Penguin Random House.

van Dernoot Lipsky, L. (2009). *Trauma Stewardship: An Everyday Guide to Caring for Self While Caring for Others.* Barrett-Koehler Publishers, Inc.

Waites, E. (1993). *Trauma and Survival: Post-Traumatic and Dissociative Disorders in Women.* W. W. Norton & Company, Inc.

Welch, E. T. (2012). *Shame Interrupted: How God Lifts the Pain of Worthlessness and Rejection.* New Growth Press.

Wiersbe, W. W. (1988). *Be What You Are.* Tyndale House Pub.

Wilson, S. D. (2001). *Hurt People Hurt People: Hope and Healing for Yourself and Your Relationships.* Discovery House Publishers.

Wilson, J. & Keane, T. (2004). *Assessing Psychological Trauma and PTSD. Second Edition.* The Guilford Press.

Zweig, C., Wolf, S. (1997). *Romancing The Shadow: A Guide to Soul Work for a Vital, Authentic Life.* Ballantine Books.

THE BLUE JEAN JACKET